PRAISE FOR *THE LONG REVOLUTION*

"Nathan Perl-Rosenthal's delightful *The Long Revolution* shows how much the story of America remains unsettled—and ours to make anew. Through his remarkably close, detailed, and ultimately inspiring study of the changing meaning of the Fourth of July, he shows how the true strength of the United States isn't in any piece of parchment, but in the thousands of small towns and big cities where decade by decade Americans made the Founders' vision their own."

—Garrett M. Graff, bestselling author of *The Only Plane in the Sky*

"By mining a trove of Fourth of July speeches delivered in our nation's first century, historian Nathan Perl-Rosenthal has unearthed some enduring preoccupations that Americans have had about their republic—their pride, their fears, their aspirations, but above all their conviction that the republic is an experiment requiring unremitting care. In a low, dishonest period in our history, this surprisingly timely book reminds us of our responsibilities."

—Mark Lilla, author of *The Once and Future Liberal*

"Nathan Perl-Rosenthal, a brilliant young historian, has figured out a way of performing a CT scan on the early

American soul: by reviewing almost 2,500 Fourth of July orations delivered during the first hundred years of the United States. The result is a memorable, and clarifying, portrait of a nation that was still figuring out what it was—an urgent project back then, and one that we might revive now."

—Nicholas Lemann, author of *Redemption*

"On the 250th anniversary of the Declaration of Independence, it is a very good idea to explore how July Fourth was celebrated in its first century. In this clever and surprising book, Nathan Perl-Rosenthal shows us that orators from all walks of life used the occasion to tell the story of the American Revolution not as something over and done but as an ongoing and unfinished transformation."

—Sophia Rosenfeld, author of *The Age of Choice*

"*The Long Revolution* is a timely and elegant national birthday present. At a time of backlash and complacency, Nathan Perl-Rosental shows us how generative and questioning the Fourth of July could be—and for whom."

—David Waldstreicher, author of *The Odyssey of Phillis Wheatley*

THE LONG REVOLUTION

Also by Nathan Perl-Rosenthal

The Age of Revolutions: And the Generations Who Made It

Citizen Sailors: Becoming American in the Age of Revolution

THE LONG REVOLUTION

CREATING A UNITED STATES AFTER 1776

NATHAN PERL-ROSENTHAL

BASIC BOOKS
New York

Cover design by Chin-Yee Lai
Cover images © GraphicaArtis/Bridgeman Images;
© MaxyM/Shutterstock.com

Basic Books
Hachette Book Group
1290 Avenue of the Americas, New York, NY 10104
www.basicbooks.com

Printed in the United States of America

First Edition: June 2026

Published by Basic Books, an imprint of Hachette Book Group, Inc. The Basic Books name and logo is a registered trademark of the Hachette Book Group.

Print book interior design by Bart Dawson.

Library of Congress Control Number: 2025046889

ISBNs: 9781541606630 (hardcover), 9781541606654 (ebook)

LSC-C

Printing 1, 2026

for S. & for E.

CONTENTS

THE LONG REVOLUTION

AN

ORATION,

DELIVERED AT

DOUGLASS, *July* 5*th*, 1802.

An orator delivering his speech on the Fourth. Frontispiece from John Crane, *An Oration Delivered at Douglass* . . . (Worcester, MA: Daniel Greenleaf, 1802). Courtesy of the Franklin Collection, Yale University Library.

INTRODUCTION

FORGET 1776

July 4, 1777: The flags waved and the cannon roared as the city of Boston celebrated the first anniversary of the United States' declaration of its independence. Militia companies mustered and marched, political leaders made toasts to the health of the newly minted nation, and ships in the harbor fired a "Grand Salute."[1]

The state legislature invited a prominent local minister, William Gordon, to deliver a discourse in honor of American independence. The British-born Gordon, who had come to North America less than a decade earlier, was a familiar figure in New England patriot circles. He was known to be "very zealous in the Cause": a strong advocate of colonial autonomy and a harsh critic of the British government. He also had a reputation for being hot tempered and loose-tongued. Inviting him to speak was always a gamble.[2]

On this occasion, Gordon delivered what his hosts had hoped for: a fierce defense of the former colonists' decision to secede from the British Empire. Riffing on the story of the "separation" of the Jewish tribes after the death of Solomon, from the Bible's Book of Kings, Gordon argued that the "Lord" was the author of revolutions. Like the North Americans of his day, the tribes had been saved from an "insulting and tyrannical" monarch by divine intervention. He exhorted his listeners to seize their chance to banish "tyranny as well as royalty out of the American states" and return them "to Europe from whence they were imported." The legislature sent a delegation later that day to ask Gordon for a copy so that it could be printed.[3]

Gordon's speech was the first Fourth of July oration to be published as a pamphlet. It would not be the last. Over the next century, between 1777 and 1876, the Fourth of July became a national festival and an essential annual occasion for debating the present and future of American politics. Orators delivered over one hundred thousand Fourth of July orations during the first century of US independence. Many were published as pamphlets, in which authors generally claimed not to have "altered the complexion of a single expression or sentiment" from how it was delivered. About twenty-five hundred of these pamphlets survive to the present day.[4]

The Fourth of July celebration with the oration as its core was an American political institution in the nineteenth century. Like the one at which William Gordon spoke in 1777, most of the celebrations were organized at the local level. Some events had official government sponsorship, but many of them were organized by political parties, advocacy groups, and professional societies. As early as the late 1780s, celebrations of the Fourth had taken on a consistent form: The day kicked off with military exercises, followed by a procession, after which crowds gathered to hear a prayer, a reading of the Declaration of Independence, and an oration. The speeches were substantial, often lasting an hour or more.[5]

The reading of the Declaration and the oration that followed it were the ritual center of the Fourth of July. Rituals are stylized reenactments of moments in a collective narrative. Like baptism in the Christian tradition, which reenacts the purification of Jesus in the River Jordan, or the Hajj, during which Muslims symbolically undertake parts of Muhammad's journeys, rituals can place their participants in communion with the person or moment being reenacted. They create a time-out-of-time, a loop in which the ritual actor connects with the original across the ocean of normal time. By reenacting how Congress had publicly proclaimed US independence in 1776, Fourth of July celebrations ritually plunged Americans back into the Revolution itself.[6]

The orations extended the ritual of the Fourth into a story. Orators did this in a limited way by narrating the events of the Revolution during the first minutes of their speeches. But their main goal, as one said in 1834, was not to recall the past but "to examine the present, and to look forward to the future." The first Fourth of July orations were modeled on speeches made for the anniversary of the so-called Boston Massacre of 1770. Orators borrowed from the long tradition of American jeremiads, speeches that used harsh criticism to incite their audiences to change and reform themselves. Speakers on the Fourth aimed to elicit feelings, to teach lessons, and to inspire action. Not by recounting the past, but by bringing the American Revolution into the present and making their listeners into actors in the revolutionary drama. Narrated in this manner, as one orator put it, the Revolution "transforms us into its own image." The twenty-five hundred published orations give us a glimpse into these fleeting annual occasions when the Revolution was renewed through repetition.[7]

The American Revolution that orators imagined and debated during the century from 1776 to 1876 was quite different from the one we think of today. Their Revolution was one still in progress. Even the event's basic boundaries in time and space remained malleable well into the nineteenth century. Its meaning, far from being settled and agreed upon, evolved repeatedly and drew radically different interpretations. And a sense of danger loomed over this long

Revolution: The threat of its failure and the nation's collapse was never far from orators' minds.

The idea that the Revolution was still underway was a major aspect of how nineteenth-century Americans perceived their political world. Americans through the Civil War regularly spoke of the Revolution not as a memory but as a continuing and still incomplete transformation. In 1791, nearly ten years after the end of the War of Independence, orator George Buchanan urged his audience to "step forward and compleat the glorious work" of the Revolution—in this case, by abolishing slavery. Fifty years later, in an oration that promoted a moral revival among his fellow citizens, Charles Hadduck declared that there were "still fetters to be broken. . . . Another Decleration of independence is to be made good; another throne to be assailed." As late as 1870, an orator in Boston could still declare that the "process" of the Revolution was "not at an end; the truths of the Declaration not being, as yet, worked out." He made this forceful statement while arguing against the then-popular idea of restricting immigration from Asia. Orators called the Revolution an "experiment": a powerful word that suggested its outcome remained uncertain, even unknowable. The long American Revolution, far from being a sepia-toned memory, was a vibrant cousin to the idea of permanent revolution that coursed through nineteenth-century European socialist and communist politics.[8]

Americans envisioned the ongoing Revolution on many geographical scales, from the town to the state, and up to the hemisphere and the globe. The long Revolution, as orators described it, was not necessarily a national event. Some viewed the Revolution's causes, course, and consequence through an expansive, global lens. Samuel Knapp rhapsodized in 1810 about how all nations were "intimately . . . connected." Revolutions in "one nation are almost always felt by others," forming a web of interconnected political upheavals. Others, such as Oliver Cobb, went in the opposite direction, entrenching themselves firmly in local contexts. Speaking in coastal Massachusetts in 1803, he credited the "hardy sons of New-England" with having spearheaded the revolutionary movement and bitterly denounced Southerners as "not . . . republican."[9] Claims about where the Revolution had taken place led to very different views of the Revolution's meaning and consequences, ranging from seeing it as an exclusively North American phenomenon to envisioning it as a universal, worldwide struggle.

Americans worried profoundly about the Revolution's fate deep into the nineteenth century. They could hardly do otherwise when they believed that the Revolution was still ongoing, its meaning still open, and its geographic borders so porous. Certainly, Fourth of July orators spouted forth their fair share of hyperpatriotic rhetoric, which was given the evocative name of "spread-eagle-ism," evoking the American emblem with its wings confidently akimbo. But such bombastic assertions of American might and unity were not the dominant theme. It was their intense doubts and anxieties about the Republic's future, as well as the legacies of the Revolution more broadly, that felt most real. This uncertainty could take on very dark tones: American political leaders regularly predicted, as one Fourth of July orator did in 1818, that the Republic would "soon be destroyed."[10]

Over the course of the century following the declaration of American independence, the idea of an ongoing revolution changed shape repeatedly, shifting in response to the evolving political landscape of the Republic.

From the formal end of the Revolutionary War in 1783 through the early years of the nineteenth century, most Americans viewed their Revolution-in-progress as a continuation of the struggle for independence. Though the Republic had been acknowledged by foreign powers, its standing on the international stage remained uncertain. Its existence was regarded, by many both inside and outside the United States, as tenuous. Political orators for decades after 1783 looked abroad with an almost obsessive intensity. They searched for signs that their republic would survive where others had not. They also could not resist comparing the American Revolution with political upheavals elsewhere. Orators usually concluded that the American Revolution was the best, but that was not always the case. Unfavorable comparisons, including to the French and Haitian Revolutions, were not unheard of.

At the start of the 1820s, Americans turned their vision of the ongoing American Revolution inward. The United States was on a more durable footing internationally and rapid economic, social, and demographic changes were creating new lines of conflict within the nation and sharpening the edge of older ones. Orators saw these disputes as so many indications that the Revolution was still not complete. They proposed competing ideas during these years about how to bring it to fulfillment. One group, reimagining the Revolution in a moralizing and individualist vein, exhorted their fellow Americans to reform their souls and morals in order to bring the Revolution to its conclusion. Others, many of whom came from groups that had previously been excluded from the orators' podium, took a more direct approach to the era's social conflicts. They characterized the era's excesses of wealth, disputes between workers and bosses, and oppression of women and minorities as signs that the Revolution's promises of equality and liberty had yet to be fulfilled.

During the two decades before the outbreak of the Civil War, from about 1840 to 1860, slavery became the unavoidable subject of American political discourse. In these years, abolitionists wielded the American Revolution as a rhetorical weapon, making it a center of their assault on the institution of slavery. Expanding and deepening the critical narratives of the Revolution articulated in earlier decades, abolitionists framed the fight against slavery as a continuation of the revolutionary struggle. In practice, this intellectual battle plan led abolitionists to be both highly critical of US society and to argue that their fellow citizens were failing entirely to conclude the revolutionary project that had begun with American independence. Nobody articulated this position with greater force than the formerly enslaved abolitionist leader Frederick Douglass, whose 1852 July Fourth speech in Rochester has justly become a classic. Yet paradoxically, the abolitionists' vision of revolutionary transformation was predicated on a sense that the Revolution was drifting away, not coming closer. They called for recommitments to the ideals of the Revolution, and the most radical among them vowed to devote themselves to its success with the same wholehearted fervor as their forefathers had done.

The climax and denouement of America's long revolution came during the Civil War and its aftermath, Reconstruction. At first, this long-anticipated explosion gave many Americans the sense that the decades separating them from the late eighteenth century had disappeared. There was a convergence—uncanny, inspiring, troubling—between the two historical moments. The Civil War, to many Americans, seemed like the Revolution come back to life. Not since the early years after the Revolutionary War had there been such a strong sense of the Revolution's immanence. Yet that also meant that when the war ended in 1865, many Americans considered it to mark the final culmination of the long revolution, the definitive closing of the revolutionary chapter in American life.

The centennial of American independence in 1876 completed the metamorphosis of the American Revolution from action into memory. That year's Fourth of July celebrations, organized for the first time at the national level, espoused a firmly memorial framing of the Revolution, shifting it squarely into the past. Not coincidentally, orators in 1876 also showed a much greater interest in Native Americans than any of their predecessors had done. Over the next decades, discussions of the Revolution felt increasingly remote. This cultural shift was mirrored in the orations' form, which became shorter and less complex, and orations were no longer printed in large numbers. Yet some still tried to hold on to the living revolutionary story. Black Americans continued to embrace the century-long belief in a Revolution-in-progress. Into the twentieth century, socialists and radicals continued, like their long-ago forebears, to cast themselves as actors in an unfinished American Revolution.

The published Fourth of July orations that form the spine of this book have considerable value as a window into the evolution of early American politics. But they also have limitations. It is important to make both explicit before delving deeper into the past as seen through them.

The advantages of the published orations as a source include the number that were printed year after year and the way they claimed to speak for large audiences. The published orations are what historians call a serial source: a type of document produced at regular intervals, in roughly similar form, containing similar kinds of information. Serial sources are useful because they provide a relatively stable "platform" from which to observe historical change at work. On average, each year from 1777 to 1875, printers published the texts of twenty-four orations. Though this represented a small share of the texts produced by American printers, the consistency of the form allows us to see how stories about the American Revolution changed over time—or remained the same. The full archive of Fourth of July orations has never been studied as a whole, though parts of it have been fruitfully examined before.[11]

Orators addressed large audiences on the Fourth, and many claimed to be speaking *for* them. Isaac Bourdeaux encapsulated this idea nicely when he described himself to his audience as their "organ" and "the interpreter of your feelings." Publishers certainly wanted their readers to believe this was the case. They often included notes from local organizers indicating that they had requested that the oration be published—as the Massachusetts legislature had done with Gordon in 1777. After 1815, growing numbers of working-class and non-white orators took to the podium on the Fourth. They presented themselves as uniquely able to represent or express their views because they shared some of these groups' experiences and characteristics. Some skepticism is warranted regarding these individuals who were trying to act as spokespeople, but their words (as historians have shown) offer one of the best ways to access the worldviews of minority and marginalized groups.[12]

Two aspects of the published orations call for caution in how we use them. One is that the vast majority of Fourth of July orations were delivered by men. The orations that were published came mostly from an even narrower group of educated, property-owning men. The published orators were by and large not famous men—many orations were the only works ever published by their authors—but neither were they average citizens. A second issue is that most of the published orations appeared in the Northeast. During the early period from 1777 to 1800, about two-thirds of published orations were delivered and printed in New England. This region was not representative of the United States as a whole, either demographically or politically.[13]

Neither of these limitations poses an insurmountable barrier to using the orations as a source for studying American political discourse. Both the identities of the orators and the regional skew of the published pamphlets were typical of the nineteenth-century print sphere writ large. Most printed materials in the period were written by men, usually elite men, and many more were printed in the Northeast than elsewhere in the country.[14] In this sense, the orations are no more biased a source than any other body of nineteenth-century printed materials. It may even be that Fourth of July oratory is less skewed than other forms of print culture. Unlike newspapers and books, the published Fourth of July orations were an offshoot of an oral practice that was present throughout the United States. It is plausible to think that the published orations represent, however imperfectly, the larger number of unpublished orations that were delivered across the length and breadth of the country.

Like William Gordon in 1777, Fourth of July orators saw it as their task to speak both to and for their communities. The stories they told about the American Revolution, in cities and towns across the United States, became an important component of the public debate about the present and future direction of the nation's politics. Orators' stories about the Revolution contributed to arguments about the emergence of the first political parties; US engagement with foreign powers and overseas entanglements; the struggle against the slave trade and the institution of slavery; fights over industrialization and the rights of working people; immigration and American expansion; and the titanic struggles over emancipation, nationhood, and the Union that erupted during the era of the American Civil War. Indeed, there was hardly any area of American politics that was not affected by the way Americans imagined their Revolution.

The story of a living Revolution, whose course could still be shaped and whose outcome remained unknown, was a powerful force in American politics during the first century after independence. The energy it generated could take Americans to quite unexpected places.

Fourth of July in Centre Square, Philadelphia, 1811–ca. 1813, attributed to Pavel Petrovich Svinin. Mixed media on paper. Courtesy of the Metropolitan Museum of Art, New York.

CHAPTER I

PLACE AND TIME

July 4, 1794: The banners fluttered, the salutes were fired, and "Citizen Alexander Macwhorter" mounted to the pulpit of Newark's Presbyterian Church to deliver an oration.

Macwhorter, an eyewitness to George Washington's crossing of the Delaware and a prominent minister in New Jersey, began his speech by marking a contrast in time. The "birth-day of kings . . . constitute, in general, the great festivals of the earth," he explained. These royal commemorations, which reminded subjects of their "degrad[ation]," were "days of sorrow not of joy." The Fourth was different, he assured his audience. It marked the start of a new "period of time, when . . . man became re-invested with . . . equal liberty."[1]

Orators like Macwhorter, who took to the podium during the first decades of the Republic's existence, narrated the story of the Revolution on a staggering variety of geographical and chronological scales. The national version that took shape during the nineteenth century—a Revolution on the Eastern seaboard, leading to US independence and an extended federal Republic—is the most familiar. But this was but one possibility among many. The Revolution could manifest in local garb, as the creation of individual cities or towns, fought out on village greens. Other orations imagined the Revolution as much bigger than the Eastern Seaboard or North America. More than a few described the Revolution as part of a continent- or Atlantic-wide process of political emancipation.[2]

The early orators proposed multiple, conflicting chronologies for the Revolution's story as well. There were those, Macwhorter among them, who conceived of it as a starting point. They saw the Revolution as the beginning of a sequence of political transformations that would stretch into the future. Others viewed the Revolution as the endpoint of a long historical process—though they disagreed about when and where it had begun. Some of them imagined the Revolution as rooted in antiquity, others in the very recent past. Many settled on telling the story of the Revolution starting with the rise of European empires in the Atlantic world, around 1500.[3]

As they imagined the Revolution spread across this dizzying diversity of times and places, orators conjured up very different kinds of events: short- or long-term, local or global, and everything in between. Their speeches contained not a single Revolution, but many.

The early orators' stories about the Revolution took shape amid intense political conflicts.

The War of Independence came to a close in 1783, after nearly eight years of hard fighting. With the Treaty of Paris, Great Britain recognized the independence of the new nation. But quiet did not follow from the peace. The states and the weak national government, governed by a fractious Congress, were heavily indebted. Bitter divisions, created and shaped by the war, persisted into the postwar era. Biological metaphors came to mind to express the fragility of the new nation. The "body politic" was in a "relaxed situation . . . after [the] violent exertions" of the war.[4] Unable to stand on its own or to control its destiny, the country and its government were in a "deplorable situation of debility."[5]

A severe economic depression and fierce political disagreements marked the first years after the war ended. The depression, caused by a toxic brew of wartime damage and postwar fiscal policies, hit the finances of the fledgling country hard. Severe shortages of hard money, among other factors, led debtors to seek legal protection from creditors—and when that failed, they turned to open revolt. In order to rein in these "democratic excesses," a group of political leaders across the colonies proposed reforming and strengthening the national government. This effort culminated in the 1787 Philadelphia Constitutional Convention. The federal constitution, which was ratified by the states in 1788 and entered into force in 1789, created a national government with the power to levy taxes, conduct foreign policy, and regulate disputes among the states and between their inhabitants.[6]

The first decade under the new national government, from 1789 to 1799, intensified the political struggle. Though early American political leaders insisted that they were opposed to factions, by 1794 Congress was split into two nascent parties, which would eventually be called Federalist and Republican. The Federalists, in broad strokes, favored government investment in infrastructure (financed by assuming debt), a strong national government wielding military force, and a rapprochement with Great Britain. Most were at least moderately antislavery. The main leaders included Alexander Hamilton and John Adams. The Republicans, aligned with France and the French Republic, supported a decentralized government, an economic policy that favored artisans and farmers and more open immigration from Europe. The Republicans were deeply divided on the question of slavery, largely but not wholly along regional lines. Their leading figures were Thomas Jefferson and James Madison.[7]

The Federalists dominated policymaking at the national level through the 1790s. The presidency, first under George Washington and then under his successor, John Adams, leaned toward the nationalist agenda championed most aggressively by Hamilton. A Federalist majority controlled Congress throughout the decade, although it slimmed after the election in 1796. The Federalists had a hammerlock on the politics of several larger states, including Massachusetts and New York. The Republicans, holding few of the levers of power, bitterly denounced their rivals and attacked their policies. The election of 1800, in which Thomas Jefferson gained the presidency and Republicans romped to power in Congress and the states, flipped the polarity of the political conflict without significantly calming it. The Democratic-Republican or Jeffersonian agenda was now dominant, at both the national and state levels. But pockets of Federalist resistance remained, especially in New England and in certain corners of Southern states, and they carried on the struggle against the Republicans with unremitting zeal after 1800.[8]

Telling the story of the Revolution on different geographic scales was one of the ways that Americans could claim the Revolution for their competing political agendas.

Fourth of July celebrations provided a perfect setting to reflect on the geography of the American Revolution. The Fourth was the most local of events, yet at the same time it insistently called upon Americans to transcend their local affiliations. The celebrations themselves were planned and executed from the bottom up. Committees of local worthies convened and set the agenda for the celebrations. The processions and ceremonies showcased local associations and institutions. In the little town of Heath, Massachusetts, one year, the procession included local militia, "Capt. Fales' Artillery" and "Capt. Leavitt's Infantry," and the ceremonies took place around "Mr. Tucker's Inn." No further details about these individuals were provided in the publication. Everyone already knew who they were. The vast majority of orators were men drawn from the local elite, individuals who had deep connections to the place. When an orator who was not a native son took to the rostrum, he would be at pains to explain and justify his place on the dais.[9]

In their speeches, orators systematically rooted the Fourth in local contexts. Sometimes the local reference was obvious, invoking revolutionary-era battles or political events. The Boston orators were the great specialists of such references, drawing liberally on the many local episodes of the imperial crisis that preceded independence. Joseph Blake, speaking in 1792, declared that he would *not* mention "the fifth of March, and nineteenth of April"—the Boston Massacre and the battles of Lexington and Concord—as a way to coyly bring them up. Other times, the reference might be a bit more oblique, as when William Smith in Charleston suggested to his audience that though there had been much suffering during the war, "the citizens of this state partook of more than their portion of the common distress." This would have been a clear allusion, for his listeners, to the violent battles that had torn through much of the South during the war. John Cushing, speaking in tiny Ashburnham, began his speech by pretending to wonder at the presence of "weapons of war" at the celebration, drawing attention to the local militia that had mustered for the occasion.[10]

Fourth of July orators combined their highly local accounts of the revolution with three other political geographies: the state, the nation, and the international scene. John McKnight provided a bravura illustration in 1794 of how to bring together these different levels. He invited his listeners to "lift up [their] eyes" and look at this "widely extended continent, from New-Hampshire to Georgia." He asked them to see in their mind's eye the various people (farmers, lawyers, merchants, and mechanics) filling "each state," each one "governed internally," and all existing harmoniously under the "general government." In the midst of this celebration of the textured unity-in-diversity of the United States, he asked them to also imagine the world abroad: to turn their eyes to "Europe," where "sparks of that fire of liberty . . . have been transported . . . and kindled into a blaze."[11] McKnight, as was typical, gave no strong indication that any one of these geographies was the central or main focus; they existed, in his oration, in a continuum.

Of course, when we think about the Revolution today we are most accustomed to thinking of the first political form of connection that McKnight evoked: the imagined unification of the various states under the "general government" of the Union. Eighteenth- and nineteenth-century orators did indeed pay attention to the notion of local communities and states all united under the aegis of the national government. Federalist Edward Gray, speaking in Boston a year after the US Constitution had entered into force, was preoccupied with the problem of unifying the states under the national government. He spent many minutes recalling the problems posed by freelancing states: "a local, not a national policy, regulated the conduct of many States." The "prosperity of a single State, and not all, was the object of its citizens." This state of affairs had been resolved by the Constitution which would, he felt confident, ensure the "union of State interests" in the "common good."[12]

Many orators, however, sought to valorize the Revolution's local dimensions rather than subordinate them to the nation, as Edward Gray had done. Perhaps resistance at the local level had provided a critical germ for the revolutionary struggle. The orator in Rochester, Massachusetts, who extolled the local people for having been "first in the contest for Freedom," was surely engaging in a bit of this imaginative play. The assertion, whether justified by the facts, served to flatter this otherwise unremarkable and mostly undistinguished locale and its people, giving them a place in the big revolutionary narrative. Jerome Smith was only being slightly less parochial when he asserted that the "Pilgrims" had "brought the seed of American liberty in the hold of the Mayflower." Speaking from a rostrum mere miles from where the Pilgrims had landed, Smith claimed for his small corner of the Massachusetts coast the honor of having been the "seed"-place of all "American liberty."[13]

A more sweeping version of this "germ" idea, in which vast phenomena grow from local "seeds," was offered up by William Jones in his 1794 oration in the town of Concord, Massachusetts. Addressing his fellow townspeople as "my countrymen," Jones recalled the battle between local militia and British regulars that took place in the town in the spring of 1775—an event usually considered to be the first battle of the Revolutionary War. "Little did you think," he went on, that this fight was the "opening of a scene . . . the dawn of that philosophy, which has since traversed the wide Atlantic." The "philosophy" that had its first outing at Concord was now poised to "inundate the whole world." Under its influence, "the princes and nobles of the earth must soon fall."[14]

Jones's vision—of the little battle of Concord setting in motion a tidal wave of transformations that would "inundate" the world—linked the town audience, in its everyday existence in rural Massachusetts, to enormous national and international events. Indeed, it unexpectedly placed these ordinary people and their little town at the center of these events. What is perhaps most notable in Jones's oration is that his vision of the scales of revolutionary activity did not end with the establishment of the United States. Indeed, he soared more or less directly from little Concord to the "wide Atlantic," and into the international revolutionary world that was in full expansion at the time of his speech.

More than a few orators explicitly rejected the idea that the nation was the appropriate container for their political sentiments. Thomas Allen, in 1803, denied that the United States was uniquely free. "Let me not be told that Civil Liberty may . . . exist in this Country" but that "in most other Countries . . . monarchical, hereditary Government, is both proper and necessary." No, he exclaimed: "In every climate and every country, the Rights of Man are the same." In 1808, the lawyer Estes Howe echoed this rejection of American exceptionalism, criticizing his countrymen who might be tempted toward excessive "love of our country." It was important to keep patriotism within "boundaries," he asserted. If patriotism were taken too far, it could "swallow up those sentiments of justice and benevolence, which we owe to mankind."[15]

The French Republic, established in the fall of 1792, was widely represented by orators—primarily, though not exclusively, those with Republican leanings—as the ultimate geographical extension of American independence. Some described the French Revolution as the natural result of the struggle for liberty in the western hemisphere. Some saw in it the fulfillment of the promise of liberation that began with American independence. Francis Blake, then a very young lawyer at the start of a distinguished career, described it thus: The United States' "glorious example, with electrical rapidity, has flashed across the Atlantic" and brought about a revolution "guided by the same principles, conducted by the same feelings." To him, the founding of the French Republic demonstrated just how powerful the revolutionary wave was: It had toppled one of the most powerful monarchies of Europe. If the American Revolution had marked the beginning of greater liberty for three million North Americans—enslaved people were not yet part of this equation, for most orators—the French Revolution was liberating many more. The French Revolution, proclaimed another orator along the same lines, "broke off the tyrant's yoke, and set free more than twenty-five million souls."[16]

The local and the national could also be imagined in opposition to each other. Timothy Hilliard, speaking in Maine (then part of the state of Massachusetts) during the early years of the nineteenth century, spent nearly a quarter of his oration on what he called "local observations." For him, it was Maine's remoteness that defined its role in the Revolution. Maine was a "detached part" of Massachusetts, far from "the seat of government, and the center of population." Because of that, it had played a limited role thus far in the revolutionary agitation. But "rapid growth" in the coming years might eventually draw it into more significant participation in the larger, national drama: "You know not what part you are to act, or what examples you are to display to your country and the world," he told his fellow Mainers, hinting at potential greatness.[17]

Orators drew sharp contrasts between different regions, which at times cut against the very idea of national unity. This was the case with Oliver Cobb, whose 1803 oration had extolled "New-England" while delivering a blistering critique of the South. Cobb, who had a "colored girl named Dinah" in his household, most likely as a servant, had strong views about slavery. "In some of our sister States," he declaimed sarcastically to his listeners—who may have included Dinah—"democracy and republicanism flourish like rice, cotton and indigo." In case any of his listeners had missed the point, he spelled it out: Any person who "oppress[ed]" slaves, he declared flatly, was "not . . . a republican."[18] For Cobb, at least, this meant that the Southern states were not properly part of the democratic-republican nation that had been created by the Revolution.

Larger spatial frames—whether global or imperial in scope—provided opportunities to draw contrasts with the revolutionary transformation in the United States. For many orators who did so, the world beyond the United States was a landscape of high contrast, all but uniformly covered in the darkness of tyranny. Samuel Bugbee, for instance, used a quarter or so of his oration to take his listeners on an imagined tour of the world and its political regimes. He invited them to look with him across Europe and see if they could "find where liberty has formed her residence." It was neither in Spain, "crushed beneath the oppressive shackles of despotism," nor in Russia, where "assassinations and oppressions alternat[ed] between prince and people." Neither would his listener find it in England. Though ostensibly a constitutional monarchy, the measures of government there left "millions starving for the necessary supports of nature"—hardly the situation of a happy and free people. Or, as another orator succinctly put it in 1814: There was only "One REPUBLIC" in the "wide world . . . and she ALONE, stands up for the universal rights of man."[19]

The British Empire provided a particularly ripe target for orators seeking a contrast abroad to the new United States. This was true of both Federalist and Democratic-Republican orators. North American colonists, when they were subjects of the British Empire, had been attentive to how the British government treated its other colonial possessions. They knew that British military and commercial policy in the Caribbean, Africa, and Asia had both direct and indirect effects on their own fate. In the wake of American independence, Americans' views of these erstwhile sister colonies evolved. They were no longer augurs of what was to come but rather cautionary tales about what might have been. Joseph Chandler asked his listeners to consider what would have become of North America had it not become independent. "We may read the answer in full grown characters imprinted with the horrid glare of . . . noble blood, in the unhappy fate of *Ireland*," he declared, and "in the despairing shrieks of the natives of *India!*"[20]

Comparisons between the United States and the wider world in this vein tended to reinforce the uniqueness of the Revolution and insist on the unity of the nation. The germinal, expansionist vision of the Revolution, which rooted it in a local context and then extended it beyond the nation's borders, had no natural resting place at the national level. Orators who deployed this image of the Revolution conceived of the North American political upheaval as a universal phenomenon, connecting the United States to foreign lands. Stories of the Revolution that contrasted it with foreign places, on the other hand, took the nation as the implicit or explicit point of comparison. This way of telling the story had the effect of reinforcing the unity of nation—as a single comparative term—and vaunting its virtues against the supposed vices of everywhere else.

Time, like place, was part of the very essence of the Fourth. So playing with chronology was another way for orators to tell very different stories about the Revolution during its early years.

The Fourth of July holiday itself was imagined as a great moment of simultaneity. Year in and year out, any number of orators began their speeches by reminding their listeners that they were celebrating at the exact same moment as others across the United States. College senior Benjamin Gleason, in 1802, loftily evoked "the incense of patriotic fervor, and affectionate gratitude [that] is rising from a thousand altars." The "shrill clarion" of "FREEDOM" was sounding "on the highest key of enjoyment, attuning the hearts of millions to the celebration."[21] The metaphor, inventively playing with the music that was a typical part of the Fourth, imagined the celebration as creating a sympathetic vibration among "the hearts of millions," all come together to celebrate at the same time.

During the years that the oratorical tradition was developing, political thinkers were also refashioning the idea of revolution and its relationship to the passage of time. Revolution in the early modern era had been used loosely to refer to all manner of rapid change, from physical sensations to the rise and fall of kings. In the late eighteenth century, "total" and "limited" revolution became the concept's two main poles. Total revolutions were imagined as ruptures in time, which "severed the connection between the past and the future," as one orator put it a few decades into the nineteenth century. Limited revolutions, more modest in their aims, sought to do away with specific ills or to restore liberties that had been lost or impaired. Orators had both concepts to hand as they narrated the American Revolution's origins and unfolding.[22]

The story of the Revolution's origins often began, for orators, in the 1750s and 1760s, during the Seven Years' War and its immediate aftermath. A common starting point was 1765's Stamp Act, a piece of British imperial legislation that had elicited howls of protest across the North American colonies. Some speakers went a bit further back, to the Albany Congress of 1754, which had taken place in the context of warfare between the colonies and Native groups. Others looked a bit later, for instance to the Boston Massacre of 1770, as the real starting gun. Yet others, while certainly admitting the relevance of these earlier dates, focused their attention more narrowly on the events of 1775 and the beginning of open war.[23]

Elijah Kellogg, a minister in Maine who had been an adolescent at the start of the Revolutionary War, was one of many who fit the Revolution into this now-familiar chronology. In an otherwise unremarkable oration delivered in 1795, he described the Revolution as a surprising but short-lived disturbance. The colonists had come to America, he said, to "enjoy the RIGHTS OF MAN." For much of the seventeenth and eighteenth centuries, they were left alone by the British government and allowed to live in freedom. The Stamp Act was "the first overt measure" by the British government to limit this liberty. The colonists' response to this event, in his narration, was an effort to rapidly restore the *status quo ante*. Only the British government's refusal to accept this, with repeated efforts to tax the colonists, kept the conflict going. By 1775, he thought, the "prospect of a reconciliation between the two countries was fast shutting [down]." (Kellogg's use of the term "country" to describe the North American colonies suggests the degree of separation he believed already existed across the Atlantic even before 1765.)[24]

Kellogg then compressed his version of the revolutionary transformation into a single year, roughly mid-1775 to mid-1776. He asserted that it was during that year that the "dispute took new ground" intellectually. What had begun as a dispute about "taxation" deepened, leading colonists (he referred to "we," without specifics) to reflect on the "true origins of" their "rights." This led Americans to move away from the traditional view that they enjoyed British liberties and toward a more radical notion of "natural rights," which granted "equality" to "equal brethren," and thus that "sovereignty, resides originally and essentially in the PEOPLE."[25] This intellectual transformation was completed with the Declaration of Independence. The Revolution, as an intellectual process, was thus, in his view, extremely rapid.

A chronology of the Revolution such as the one that Kellogg proposed led readily to the conclusion that the Revolution was a closed parenthesis. After all, if it had begun so suddenly—as an abrupt irruption of discord into an otherwise peaceable situation—it was natural to think it had concluded just as abruptly, or, in any event, that the peaceable situation of the before-times would reassert itself. This was exactly what Kellogg thought had happened. His brief account of the war ended with a rapid reestablishment of harmony: "Having weathered the storm, and made our port, we dropped anchor, and turned in for rest." The concerns of the postwar period led to the Constitutional Convention, which would in his view resolve all possible conflicts; it would ensure that the United States was "forever improving, without tumult, or the hazard of a revolution."[26]

Many orators in the early Republic, however, began their narrations of the Revolution long before the 1760s. In the first minutes of their orations, they would glance back at the Middle Ages or the very beginning of the early modern era in the fifteenth and sixteenth centuries. These extended chronologies imagined the American Revolution as a recent, albeit very significant, expression of a long-unfolding process of liberty's development and self-revelation. Some orators reached so far back into the past that their stories became deep time histories of the American Revolution. John Phillips, in the mid-1790s, took several minutes at the outset of his oration to expound on the "distant causes" of the Revolution. Phillips clearly suspected that the history of liberty, of which the Revolution was part, reached all the way back to antiquity—to the struggles for freedom in Greece and Rome. But he felt that it was impossible to perceive clearly what had happened in antiquity, so he contented himself with starting the story of the Revolution with the "birth of European empires." In his account, the first English settlers in North America had the "noblest of motives, the attainment of civil and religious liberty," and in order to secure it they created "literary institutions" that spread "knowledge" among the populace. This, he argued, had rendered the revolution all but inevitable. Phillips's modesty about his ability to know the past was not universally shared. Joseph Chandler, speaking a few years later in Monmouth, Maine, where he served as a minor official, devoted a quarter of his oration to recounting a history of liberty, leading into the American Revolution, that began from the creation of the world as told in the Bible.[27]

Histories of resistance to oppression over centuries, with the American Revolution as their continuation, were another oratorical commonplace. Isaac Watts Crane, speaking in Newark, New Jersey, began his oration with an excursus on the "oppressed and fugitive" ancestors of Americans. They had "for many years previous to the revolution, discover[ed] an uniform disposition to govern themselves," and a consistent rejection of all "arbitrary acts." This genealogy positioned the American Revolution as merely the most recent flowering of a centuries-old tree of resistance. Even more vehement on the subject was Paul Allen, who in 1806 denounced the idea that "the birth of American Liberty was coeval . . . with the birth of her Independence." He argued strenuously that their "fathers" had been steeped in "the sturdy habits of Republicanism" from the sixteenth century onward. The American colonists, he summarized bluntly, "were always free." Anyone who says otherwise "spits . . . venom on the grave of his ancestors."[28]

These accounts of revolutionary time, which described the Revolution as occurring within a long and deep chronological frame, made it easy to envision the American Revolution as an ongoing event. If it had been going on for a long time already, after all, it was perfectly plausible to imagine it as continuing. Jonathan Loring Austin, delivering the Boston oration in 1786, insisted that the Revolution's energies were not yet spent and that its mission was still underway. The nation's "feelings" remained aroused, he declared; the "enlivening spark, the generous ardour still glows in every bosom." He listed a long agenda of tasks that his fellow citizens still had to accomplish, ranging from the physical rebuilding of towns to guaranteeing payment of wartime loans. In this case, the idea that the Revolution's work was incomplete may have had a self-interested dimension: Austin, a successful businessman, had spent part of the Revolutionary War years on a mission in Europe to secure a loan for the state of Massachusetts. Like many who served in such capacities, he may still have been owed money that he hoped to collect.[29]

Drawing on these longer chronologies, Americans across the political spectrum endorsed the idea that the Revolutionary War had been just one step in a longer process. For the poet and arch-Republican Joel Barlow, in 1787, the revolution was at best "half completed." Indeed, he suggested that the harder part remained to be accomplished. Americans had "contended with the most powerful nation . . . now we have to contend with ourselves." In this struggle, nothing less than the country's "existence" was at stake. A similar kind of message was still being delivered six years later. The minister Samuel Deane imagined the United States as an infant nation that still had far to go before it assumed anything like its final form. "That which is born must be carefully nurst, if we wish it to arrive to maturity and masculine vigour." Five years later, in 1798, Federalist Josiah Quincy was still striking similar notes. "Let no man persuade himself that . . . Independence be preserved without arduous conflicts," he warned.[30] Fifteen years after the treaty that ended the Revolutionary War had been signed, the fight for autonomy was still far from over in his eyes.

The vision of the Revolution as yet to be accomplished, and as an ongoing process in time, took its strongest form in the orators' visions of the future. Rare was the orator who did not at least gesture into the unknown. Many made it a central destination of their discourse. William Linn, speaking in New York in 1791, contemplated a time "not far distant, when tyranny every where shall be destroyed." He pointed to the French Revolution as a key agent of this prospective transformation. Though the "flame" of the French Revolution had not been kindled by Americans alone, "we contributed to blow and increase it, as France will in other nations." Eventually, with "blaze joining blaze," the "remotest corners of the earth" will be overtaken by the revolutionary fires, he predicted. Nearly forty years later, an orator in Burlington, Vermont, looked forward to "the day, which we hope is not distant," when the Revolution would be "consummated" for all "mankind."[31] In this vision, the American Revolution marked the beginning of an extended sequence of similar revolutionary moments that stretched into the years to come.

Accordion-like, the Revolution expanded and contracted in both time and space as orators narrated it on the Fourth. Sometimes, they spread the Revolution far and wide. They might begin its story centuries or even millennia in the past, or imagine its sparks igniting continents or the entire globe.

Other orators, at different moments, made the Revolution seem small by emphasizing its local causes or limiting its scope to a few short years. No single version was entirely dominant. But certain notes sounded more strongly and more frequently than others. The idea that the Revolution was not limited to North America was quite widespread. So too was the notion that the Revolution's origins reached back at least a century or more. These contributed to a consensus that the Revolution was bigger than just North America and the former British colonies—though beyond that point, agreement became more elusive.

Different versions of the Revolution's story supplied arguments for partisans' competing political agendas. Though typically imagined as an occasion for unity and consensus—a "civic rite of communal reverence"—the Fourth of July during these early years was a prime occasion to pursue political disagreements. The Democratic-Republicans, who favored good relations with France, told stories of the American Revolution that connected it organically to France and the French Revolution. Many of them viewed the Revolution as an expansive and forward-looking movement whose endpoint was difficult to predict; they appreciated thinking of it as an ongoing transformation. Federalists, who were more inclined to align closely with Great Britain, emphasized the English or British origins of revolutionary ideals, rooting the Revolution in practices brought over by colonists from England. Federalists were also more inclined to imagine the Revolution as a finished or nearly completed transformation, the better to reestablish order and hierarchy in the new nation. Yet these versions of the Revolution did not have fixed partisan meanings; they remained flexible and open to reinterpretation.[32]

With its meaning the subject of tremendous disagreement and its geographic and temporal contours in flux, the Revolution could hardly form a stable foundation on which Americans might build a nation or a single national consciousness. The unfinished quality and protean shape of the Revolution, as orators retold it, made it more than uncertain. It became a source of fear and worry for orators and their audiences. For the Revolution, unstable and uncertain as it was, seemed in perpetual danger of imminent collapse.

FOURTH OF JULY!

A meeting of the citizens of Brandon was held at the Inn of A. W. Titus, on the 18th of June, when it was resolved that the approaching Anniversary of our

National Independence

should be appropriately commemorated, and that our fellow citizens of the *adjoining towns* be invited to join in such *celebration.*

COL. DAVID WARREN, ***of Brandon,*** **was** designated as the Chief Marshal of the day, and the following gentlemen were appointed Aids:—Ward M. Lincoln, Drances June, David S. Murray, and *J. D.* Mitchell of Brandon, and John Capen of Goshen; and the following were appointed Deputy Marshals:—Sam'l S. Crooks of Salisbury, Elnathan Knapp of Goshen, S. D. Townsend of Pittsford, S. St. John of Hubbardton, Enoch Smith, jr. of Sudbury, Jos. Simonds of Whiting, Silas Johnson of Leicester, and Dan B. Bogue of Chittenden.

The undersigned were appointed a Committee of Arrangements, and they respectfully invite their fellow citizens to join the inhabitants of Brandon in celebrating the ever-memorable Fourth of July. The Deputy Marshals will take charge of the delegations from their respective towns, and report themselves to the Chief Marshal, at Titus' Inn, by 10 o'clock on the morning of the day. The Oration wil be pronounced at 11 o'clock, A. M.

A salute of 26 guns will be fired at sunrise and at sunset.

Provision will be made for the accomodation and comfort of Revolutionary Soldiers, who are earnestly invited to attend.

A place in the proceedings is assigned to 26 young ladies, representing our Federal Union.

WM. M. FIELD, DAVID WARREN, DRANCES JUNE, CALVIN P. AUSTIN, FREEMAN R. FORBES, DAVID S. MURRAY, VOLNEY ROSS, E. W. WINSLOW,	Committee of Arrangements.	WARD M. LINCOLN, E. J. BLISS, E. N. BRIGGS, D. W. C. CLARKE, EDW'D JACKSON, C. W. CONANT, A. W. TITUS, CHARLES BACKUS.

A broadside announcing a Fourth of July celebration in 1830. Courtesy of the Library of Congress, Rare Book and Special Collections Division, Printed Ephemera Collection.

CHAPTER 2

DOUBTS

July 4, 1810: Across the country, the flags waved, the cannon roared, and for the thirty-fourth anniversary of the Declaration of Independence, orators climbed the steps to their perches in the late morning to deliver their discourses.

Many orators struck dark and pessimistic notes on what should have been a happy day. "The hour is mournful and the prospect gloomy," declared lawyer Samuel Knapp. Since the spring of 1803, Britain and Napoleon's France had been at war—a conflict that was consuming Europe and the Atlantic world. In the face of this, Knapp wished that Americans would redouble their efforts to preserve the US's independence and the liberty it conferred. Instead, he felt, they were "gazing in stupid wonder at the gigantic strides" made by Napoleon, the "destroyer," and failing to react. The British government, which was trying to compel the United States to take its side in the war, did not seem much better in his eyes.[1]

The grim tone of Knapp's oration was not unusual. Since the 1780s, a hefty share of Fourth of July oratory had had a pessimistic tinge. It was not that orators did not find much to celebrate in the American Republic. They did. An attentive listener to Fourth of July speeches from 1777 to 1810 would have regularly heard praise for George Washington, the Constitution, certain political leaders, and the hard work, virtue, and religiosity of North Americans. Yet all these achievements seemed to be overshadowed by danger. For at least the first thirty years after independence, orators consistently expressed serious doubts about whether the Republic would endure.

Americans' strong conviction that the Revolution was an unfinished process was the intellectual source of this uncertainty. This conviction took shape most forcefully in the language of "experiment," a term that surfaced regularly in public discourse during the era of the early Republic. Though already present in the early 1790s, "experiment" became a regular part of the oratorical tool kit after Thomas Jefferson used it in his 1801 inaugural address. Fourth of July orators asserted that the United States and its government were "experiments" that were still underway. Though at times they deployed this language with the intention of arguing that it was a grand adventure—as Jefferson had done—they more often used this framework to argue that the Revolution and the country it had created remained unfinished and vulnerable.

The fragility of the United States was brought home to Americans by orators in two main ways: through reflections on the fortunes of foreign republics and comments on the passing of the revolutionary generation. Fourth of July orators were highly attentive to the links between the United States and the wider world. Many viewed the Revolution and the political community it had created as extending beyond the boundaries of North America. Yet the record of republican governments in the era was not reassuring. Wherever they looked, orators found republics that had fallen into crisis, like those in South America, or that had been swallowed up by empires or devoured by conflict, as in France. Looking inward, orators found something equally disturbing: the signs of an inevitable yet worrisome generational shift as veterans of the Revolutionary War passed away. Their departure left the United States bereft of its staunchest defenders.

By any measure, American independence remained a work in progress for decades after Congress issued its "unanimous Declaration" in July 1776. The 1783 Treaty of Paris ended the war, but Britain continued to have plans for dominating

North America. As one orator put it, Britain's acknowledgment of American independence was more in the nature of "an armistice . . . than a peace."[2]

The postwar economic crisis and the decision to revise the framework of the national government that produced the US Constitution were seen as continuations of the independence struggle. In a thundering defense of the new Constitution in 1788, Enos Hitchcock, a minister who had served as a chaplain during the Revolutionary War, declared that a "REVOLUTION can never be considered as complete till government is firmly established." Joseph Blake, speaking in Boston in 1791, envisioned the writing of the Constitution as a continuation of the war itself.[3]

Public confidence in the safety of American independence remained fragile at best during the 1790s. Many Americans greeted the beginning of the French Revolution in 1789 as a natural and happy result of the American revolt. Even some who would later become fierce critics initially celebrated a movement that had freed "more than twenty millions of people" and raised them "to the dignity and happiness of freedom, and Independence." Orators thought they recognized in France the "influence" of the American Revolution, imagined as a "practical lesson of liberty to mankind." Yet as the French Revolution turned against the monarchy and became militarized starting in 1792, Americans' fears resurged. Samuel Deane cautioned against "pusilanimity and contemptible weakness" in the face of French aggression. Josiah Quincy warned in 1798 that there was no way that "Independence [could] be preserved without arduous conflicts."[4]

The turn of the nineteenth century brought a change of focus without any significant diminution in the overall tone of alarm. France and Britain were engaged in a seemingly interminable war, during which these well-matched powers disputed the dominance of Europe and the globe, including swaths of the North American continent to the west and north of the United States. Even if armed invasion by either power was unlikely, each side aimed to force the United States into its camp. French and British agents nurtured many "internal broils" and "angry divisions" within the country. Orators warned in dark terms about the "arts of deception" that always threatened to destroy "free states," and hinted that such "deceptions" were growing unchecked in the heart of the nation.[5]

The War of 1812 shattered whatever limited confidence Americans had managed to acquire over the previous decades in the security of the United States. The new war between Britain and the United States broke out after years of growing tensions between the two countries, largely due to disputes concerning shipping and sailors. The conflict sparked a fresh outpouring of concern about the safety and durability of American independence. Rollin Mallary, speaking near the nadir of US fortunes in the war, strenuously called for the defense of what he referred to as the "last of republics." The implication that even the American Republic might not exist for much longer was hard to avoid.

An orator in Worcester, Massachusetts, in 1814 fretted that unless Americans united in their defense, “we shall forfeit in this war whatever glory” the United States had gained in the War of Independence. “The very infancy of our republic may . . . be the only part of its history worth remembering!” Even in 1815, after the war had ended on fairly favorable terms for the United States, orators continued to worry that the “British” still “treat those with contempt who bear the name of Americans.”[6]

The sense of uncertainty that permeated the public imagination around the turn of the nineteenth century was encapsulated by orators’ description of the Republic as an “experiment.”

The language of experiment first appeared in a published Fourth of July oration in 1792. Joseph Blake Jr., one of the younger men yet invited to give the official Boston oration, invoked this language while discussing the federal Constitution. He declared that he was going to skip the “fashionable” practice of making intricate comparisons between the Constitution’s provisions and those in other frames of government. “Experiment,” he declared, is the only way to “prove the perfection of political institutions.” He thus juxtaposed “experiment,” meaning the process of living with and putting into action a framework of government, to theoretical analysis. In so saying, Blake picked up an already familiar theme in orations, which would become ever more popular as the decade went on: the notion that American politics was more practical and grounded in experience than that of other places.[7]

Thomas Jefferson's first inaugural address in 1801 brought the language of experimentation into wide usage. In the first minutes of the speech, he addressed those who "fear that a republican government can not be strong." "Would the honest patriot," he asked rhetorically, "in the full tide of successful experiment, abandon a government which has so far kept us free . . . ?"[8]

Experiment was no idle word in the late eighteenth century—especially not for the scientifically minded Jefferson. Experimental science took root in the Anglo-American world during the second half of the seventeenth century. Leading English natural philosophers, such as the chemist Robert Boyle, proposed it as a new way of knowing things. Instead of knowledge coming from textual authority or long-hallowed tradition, it would be based on empirical demonstrations that provided proof of principles. Experiments were central to this new way of knowing. It was experiments, observed by reliable witnesses, that created confidence in one's understanding of how the physical world worked.[9]

The "experimental life" was a world of permanent uncertainty and curiosity. By its very nature, experimental knowledge is an approximation of the truth or reality. Logical deductions from first principles provide complete certainty—assuming that all the premises are correct and the reasoning is sound. Experiments are different. An experiment is, by definition, site- and moment-specific: It takes place in a laboratory, in a field, or wherever the experimentalist makes it happen. The conditions there, from weather to other factors, matter in determining how it turns out. The relationship between this single demonstration and the larger principle, then, must be actively created: The experiment must be reliably witnessed or recorded, its significance must be explained, and its validity as a demonstration of the principle or theory must be argued. Each of these steps contains uncertainty about its result and its meaning.[10]

Jefferson, that masterful artisan of opaque phrases, loosely colored the scientific concept onto a political canvas. What did it mean to call the United States an "experiment"? It suggested that the American Republic was site-specific: The "experiment" underway here, like other experiments, was taking place in a particular and distinctive location. It was also a trial, an essay in the old-fashioned sense of the word: Americans were trying out this political form, seeing how it worked. The final results were as yet unknown—though Jefferson optimistically embraced the idea that it had thus far been "successful."

Orators on the Fourth quickly picked up on this language. A handful made the borrowing explicit by quoting Jefferson directly. One 1803 orator even put "successful experiment" in quotation marks in the published version of his remarks. The reference had considerable staying power:

As late as 1829, an orator could still quote the entire phrase "the full tide of successful experiment." They did not even lose track of the word's scientific connotations. When the nineteenth-century theatrical star Edwin Forrest delivered a rip-roaring oration in New York City in 1838, he cited both Isaac Newton and Benjamin Franklin as proof that "it was experiment that gave this hemisphere to the world. It was EXPERIMENT that gave this continent FREEDOM." American orators' fondness for the language of experiment was genuinely unusual; it was uncommon, if not altogether unknown, in the parallel French and South American republican traditions.[11]

Most orators made a freer and more expansive use of Jefferson's notion of experimentation. Few, in any event, dared to leave it as ambiguous as Jefferson had. What, precisely, was this "experiment"? The most common approach was to speak of an "experiment of self-government," or some version of that phrasing. This emphasized the experimental nature of a government in which "the people" were sovereign. This was an experiment not in the sense that it had not been attempted—it had been, from antiquity onward—but in the sense that it had never quite succeeded. Wherever the "great experiment of Republicanism" had been "tried," one orator observed, it had "failed." The super-Federalist William Cunningham wondered aloud, in 1803, whether the American experiment "would be . . . successful." About a decade later, at a Fourth of July celebration sponsored by the now much reduced Federalist camp, one of the speakers called for undertaking the "noble and generous . . . experiment" of ending party strife—even though he suspected that any such effort was doomed to "fail."[12]

Some orators opened the frame of "experiment" wide—as wide as the idea of freedom itself. There is a "great experiment of freedom . . . going on in this country," declared one orator two years after the end of the War of 1812. Another, in 1823, hailed the Fourth as the anniversary of the start of a "bold and hazardous experiment of erecting among us a free and equal government." Freedom could refer to much more than just self-government. It could mean the exercise of rights, the ability to worship according to one's conscience, the choice of a career.[13] Describing all these aspects of American life as part of an "experiment"—and a "hazardous" one at that—transformed the very essence of the American revolutionary achievement, not just the forms of government it had created, into a question mark.

Others located the heart of the "experiment" in narrower, arguably safer confines. The historian George Bancroft, in an oration in the mid-1820s, called the "system of states an experiment" in different styles and forms of government, which allowed citizens by "mutual observation" to identify the "best" one. An 1835 orator in Danville, Kentucky, described the 1787 Constitution as "an experiment in politics, as unprecedented as the voyage of Columbus was in navigation." By the time the Constitution was enacted, all the states already had republican self-government. The originality of the Constitution, and thus its "experimental" character, was that it created a republican national government that spanned a large territory, and federated the individual state-republics underneath it.[14]

Although most orators followed Jefferson in giving a positive spin to the idea of an experiment, a few took the concept in the opposite direction. John Quincy Adams, the future president and forceful advocate of a strong national government, succinctly dismissed the pre-Constitution national government in 1831 as an "experimental and imbecile" construct. In a fierce address delivered in 1834, Black minister Joseph M. Corr used the language of experimentation to denounce colonization, a then-fashionable plan to send free African Americans to Africa. Colonization, though favored by some abolitionists as a way to gradually and peacefully bring about the end of slavery in the United States, was firmly opposed by many Black thinkers and activists. He called it a "soul and body destroying experiment . . . [the] handmaid of slavery." At a partisan Fourth of July celebration that took place in Portland, Maine, a few years later, John Appleton denounced the Alien and Sedition Acts of 1798 as a "mad . . . experiment upon the American People." Similar laws, Appleton warned darkly, had led to the outbreak of recent revolutions in Europe.[15]

Regardless of how exactly they formulated it, orators who invoked the idea of experimentation cloaked the Republic in a veil of ongoing uncertainty. "It becomes us still to regard our government in light of an experiment," said Alexander Brown in Pittsburgh, "and not to be too confident of its ultimate success." This was in 1842, after more than sixty-five years of independence. Or, as Horace Mann put it that same year—with perhaps a bit less skepticism—the American Republic had no prior models to serve as guides. With "no experience . . . derived from similar experiments, to guide us," he summed up, all Americans could do was "grope where we cannot see."[16] This was not as dark a vision of the country's future as the one put forward by Brown. But it expressed a deep uncertainty nonetheless.

Americans' worries about the fate of the republican "experiment" within the United States were heightened when they looked abroad. During the first decades of the Republic's existence, virtually every Fourth of July oration included a discussion of some length regarding foreign powers and international politics. At issue was how the United States compared to other types of states and what lessons could be drawn from these foreign analogies about the fate of the United States. On the whole, the lessons were not reassuring.

Reflections on foreign politics held a prominent place in Fourth of July speeches. On average, orators devoted some fourteen percent of the total length of their addresses in the late eighteenth and early nineteenth centuries to discussions of foreign places. The actual weight that orators gave to foreign politics varied widely, ranging from sidelong comments to elaborate disquisitions that occupied nearly the entire oration. But as one of them put it, "a comparative view of this our glorious revolution" was a constant in the speeches. Orators typically staged their examinations of contemporary foreign politics with the help of a two-part backdrop, composed of brief but telling historical remarks on Native Americans and classical Greece and Rome.[17]

Native America served as one part of the historical framing for orators' commentaries on the broader revolutionary world. During the early decades after independence, populous and increasingly well-armed Native nations living on the borders of the new Republic posed the most immediate geopolitical challenge to the United States on the continent. Their territorial sovereignty, which extended over entire regions that the United States claimed as its own, limited Americans' ability to move. Native nations' long-standing treaty relations with European powers made American statesmen fearful that these nations could collaborate with the US's overseas competitors to permanently constrain the new Republic. Orators expressed these fears of Native power in passages that denounced their "savage" behavior and dwelled on the role of Native warriors as British allies in the Revolutionary War.[18]

Most Fourth of July orators, however, found it more useful for their purposes to transform Native peoples into symbols of the past—while simultaneously making them disappear in the present. In 1803, orators in West Springfield, Massachusetts, and Beaufort, South Carolina, speaking almost simultaneously, invoked Native Americans as symbols of bygone colonial history, which had now been "supercede[d]" by the United States. By the 1820s, orators were using an explicitly eliminationist rhetoric. One described triumphantly how the "white man" had swept away the "Indian" who had lived there for "an hundred generations," building "temples, colleges and churches" on what had been their land. Sharp-tongued young David Daggett, who would later become a prominent jurist and a founder of Yale Law School, was one of the few orators who took a more critical view of Americans' treatment of Native peoples. In 1787, he told his audience that their ancestors had "forcibly or fraudulently depriv[ed] the natives of their possessions." Yet even he said these things merely as a prelude, a segue into a harangue criticizing his fellow citizens for their moral failings in the present.[19]

The history of the classical-era republics of Greece and Rome formed a second, more elaborate backdrop to orators' remarks on contemporary politics. The ancient republics had been a favorite topic of contemplation for European political thinkers from the Renaissance onward. Various intellectual traditions addressed the question of classical republicanism. The dominant one was shaped by the Florentine politician and scholar Niccolò Machiavelli and his intellectual heirs. These thinkers drew on the Greek historian Polybius to understand the history and practice of government. Polybius framed his studies of ancient history around two opposing forces: the tendency of all forms of government to "decay" or decline, and the capacity of human beings to act to sustain them.[20]

For Polybius's early modern students, the key to preserving governments in the face of their inevitable decline was the "virtue" of citizens. "Virtue" meant a specific kind of economic, moral, and intellectual positioning based largely on the ownership of property. The propertied man, because he was economically independent, was understood to be invested in the fate of government and to enjoy a degree of autonomy in thought and judgment. The combination of autonomy and investment meant that the virtuous, propertied citizen was in a unique position to govern the state. The early eighteenth century theorist Henry Bolingbroke influentially described the English gentry as being the central repository of virtue in the English political system, and thus the guarantors of its stability.[21]

During the decade-long imperial crisis that led to the declaration of American independence, North American politicians dwelled obsessively on the classical republics. Pamphlets, newspapers, and public discourse burst with learned references to the histories of Greece and Rome. They were particularly focused on the conditions that had led to the collapse of regimes of "liberty": the Roman Republic, in particular, but also the appearance of tyrannical regimes in the Greek city-states. As had been the case for much of the previous three centuries, however, these discussions of ancient republics were essentially theoretical: While North American thinkers might believe that ancient history had lessons to offer, they were well aware of the differences between ancient and modern times. Their view of this republican past was also colored by monarchism: Like most of their predecessors, they espoused a republicanism modified to fit a world still dominated by monarchical governments. A state without a king at its head was not merely undesirable for them; it was virtually unthinkable.[22]

For Fourth of July orators, the question of republicanism was no longer a scholarly or abstract one—and it was no longer limited to an examination of ancient antecedents. The independence of the United States, under a kingless republican form of government, gave an urgency and immediacy to the question that it had lacked for much of the previous three centuries. By the middle of the 1780s, the United States was no longer alone as a republic on the world stage: The American Revolution, one orator declared, had "regenerated the world." Beginning with attempts to overthrow the oligarchical government of the Dutch Republic in 1780 and continuing with unrest in the Swiss Confederation, a republican ferment began nearly as soon as American independence had been declared. Over the next four decades, orators had an increasingly dense and complex matrix of republican experiments to think with.[23]

France was a chief focus of Fourth of July orators during the first half century of American independence. The American relationship with France and the French during these decades was ambiguous. At one pole was a sense of gratitude for the essential assistance that the French monarchy under Louis XVI had provided to the United States during the Revolutionary War against Britain. Even Francophobic orators had to admit that without the assistance of the French Navy and French financing, the struggle for independence would almost certainly have failed.[24] Yet this gratitude was mixed with suspicion and a measure of hostility. The long-standing animosity between Britain and France, which most Anglo-Americans had imbibed practically with their mothers' milk, was not easily overcome.

The crisis of the French monarchy in 1787 and 1788, along with the outbreak of revolution in 1789, brought North Americans' interest in France to a fever pitch. American observers watched the progress of the revolution in France with a searing attention. Orators celebrated the seizure of the Bastille and the creation of the National Assembly in 1789, which brought an end to the king's absolute power. Many were equally comfortable celebrating the republican turn that occurred in 1792, when the king was deposed and a republic declared. "We remember with horror the continued effusion of blood, which darkened the morning of their revolution," said one. But he was quick to blame this sanguinary turn on the "treachery of a tyrant." "FRENCHMEN," he called out, "Be firm, be undaunted in the struggle." Another celebrated the "heroic and unconquerable republicans" who had executed the "important revolution in France . . . so justly celebrated for the magnitude of its object."[25]

In the years after 1789, a number of orators offered full-throated endorsements of the French Revolution on the Fourth. Merchant Archibald Buchanan, speaking in

Baltimore, Maryland, in 1794, after reminding his audience of France's indispensable aid to the American Revolution, was unrestrained in his praise of the country's revolution. "Fight on . . . illustrious nation," for the "glorious cause" of "philosophy, reason, and liberty." Even the execution of the former king, Louis Capet, did not trouble him too much. Yes, he admitted, it was regrettable that Louis had been put to death. But it was necessary for the revolution to progress and (in case there was any ambiguity remaining), "I cannot help rejoicing . . . that he has fallen." Another orator that same year, Joseph Clark, though somewhat less fulsome in his enthusiasm for the French Revolution, still had high praise for it. France, that "benign friend of the human race," had thoroughly embraced "the genius of Liberty" and was now triumphing rapidly over "those countries . . . under the dark clouds of despotism." Clark foresaw that France would not "stop . . . till she has brought all her enemies under her feet."[26]

Celebrations of France and the French Revolution were increasingly tempered by hesitations about the fragility of its republican government and its imperial ambitions. As revolutionary and then Napoleonic France extended its power over Europe and beyond, starting in the late 1790s, the tone of the commentary darkened. The French Revolution had been viewed as a child of the American Revolution, as a continuation of it; it now came to be seen as a new cautionary tale. "Behold in Europe, a new Empire . . . pressing forward . . . to universal dominion," declaimed the Boston orator in 1798. Though the government in Paris was still republican in form, the orator Josiah Quincy Jr. doubted the sincerity of its commitments: It had only a "specious pretence of giving liberty and rights," he sneered. Others doubted whether there was really much difference anymore between the various "parties" in Europe, and they congratulated the United States on its decision to maintain an "equal neutrality" with respect to both Britain and France.[27]

For some, the French Revolution became a counterexample, whose differences from the American Revolution had to be underscored. Jonathan Ellis, in the early nineteenth century, made one such sharp and explicit comparison between the American and French Revolutions. The "change" that took place during the American Revolution, he argued, "differs much from a revolution, in the more modern use of the word"—by which he meant the French Revolution. "We [Americans] contended for the preservation and perpetuity" of rights; "we did not seek the overthrow and destruction of any system of government," as had the French.[28] Because in his view Americans already had liberty, and sought only to "preserv[e]" it, their revolution was limited. The French, in his view, sought a much more open-ended, total transformation of the political order.

Starting in the second decade of the nineteenth century, orators focused their speeches on South America. Napoleon Bonaparte's conquest of Spain in 1808 had unleashed a cascade of political crises in Spanish America. In much of South America, local authorities in the disrupted empire claimed power in the name of the Spanish monarch and the people. While most of the early revolts claimed to be working in the monarch's interest, republican flames began to burn widely in 1810, particularly in the northern regions of the continent. By 1814, a number of fragile republican regimes had taken root, especially in present-day Colombia and Venezuela.[29]

Orators saw in South America close echoes of the United States' own struggles. "Their cause ought to excite our sympathies . . . for they are now, as we once were," declared Leonard Parker in 1816. He urged his listeners to "cherish the hope" that South America would eventually become a "sister republic" to the United States. A few years later, another orator in Boston insisted that Americans "cannot be indifferent" to the "great struggle going on in South America." For, he declared, they are "struggling for the same rights that we have . . . obtained." Unlike when they spoke about the French Revolution, orators discussed the South American revolutions as a promise or work in progress rather than a fulfillment or model. Yet the fate of the whole "march of freedom" was bound up in the outcome of each individual struggle.[30]

After the initial excitement about South American republicanism began to fade in the mid-1820s, the public imagination took a more critical turn. South America became an object lesson in the degradation of republican forms of government that so haunted orators' dreams about the United States. In region after region, from Chile to Mexico, republican governments in Spanish-speaking America proved unstable and all too susceptible to falling under the sway of authoritarian rulers. The case of northern South America, specifically the region of Gran Colombia, was particularly concerning to North American observers. This area had produced some of the earliest republican declarations after 1808. Though formally a republic, Colombia was dominated by the military leader Simón Bolívar. In the Río de la Plata and Mexico, republican forms coexisted with dictatorial and oligarchic forms of governance.[31]

In their French and South American comparisons—as well as references to other contemporary revolutions, especially in Greece—orators made an ambiguous assertion about the wider republican world within which the United States existed. Their negative characterizations of contemporary republics as fragile and unstable cast a positive light on the relative durability of the United States. Yet their dark prognostications about these other republics could not help but reinforce the idea that all republics—including the United States—were innately fragile structures liable to crumble at any moment.[32]

Orators were also capable of reaching for republican comparisons that directly put the United States in a less favorable light. Orville Luther Holley, a newspaper editor, made the unlikely decision to offer an extensive celebration of the Haitian Revolution in an 1822 oration delivered in upstate New York. The title itself of his oration summed up the anxiety that Americans still felt, nearly fifty years after independence, about the stability of their country: "An Oration, On the Permanency of Republican Institutions." (An excerpt is on pp. 195–198.) Holley argued that for institutions to endure, they had to coincide with and have the support of "the character of the communities which live under them."[33]

Having surveyed republics from antiquity to the present, Holley turned to Haiti, which he praised immoderately. The Haitians had established "republican" institutions, he argued, and the success of these institutions, in spite of widespread hostility from European powers, was the result of the "energetic genius" of their leaders and the way they had "cultivated" self-improvement. He predicted that soon all of the Caribbean islands "shall be revolutionized" and their "wealth and power . . . transferred to the negroes." His encomium to Haiti contained more than a grain of reproach against his North American brethren, whom he accused of being blind to the humanity of the African Americans they enslaved.[34]

Unlike the discussions of South America or the French Republic, Holley's soliloquy on Haiti did not explicitly stress the fragility of republican forms of government. On the contrary, he argued that given the progress of liberty in a place like Haiti, it was likely that the United States, which had given the initial "lesson" of liberty to the world, would continue to progress. But even Holley seemed to have difficulty believing his own breezy assurance that the American Republic would endure. Even he had to admit that Americans had "not advanced as rapidly in moulding our character and sentiments into perfect conformity to the spirit of our institutions."[35] The comparison to Haiti, as had been the case with comparisons to the republics of Europe and South America, ended on a suspensive note of uncertainty.

The theoretical debate about the fragility of US sovereignty during its early decades took place amid a more concrete manifestation of the revolution's fragility: the passing of the revolutionary generation.

It was a commonplace of Fourth of July celebrations for the orator to look out over the audience and single out the men who were old enough to be veterans of the war against Britain. Sometimes these individuals were known directly to the orator or made themselves known through distinctive dress or banners. John Lathrop in the mid-1790s saw "many of the illustrious remnant of that band of patriots" in the crowd. But just as often, orators simply guessed at the presence of veterans based on their age. As Isaac Bourdeaux said, while speaking to a crowd in South Carolina, "In this assembly perhaps I behold the venerable countenances of some of our earliest patriots."[36]

The presence of veterans at Fourth of July celebrations mattered to orators and audiences because they provided a direct link to the experience of the revolutionary conflict. William Hobby noted that "those who were engaged in the seven years following war can recollect better than language can describe" the "feelings by which they were personally influenced" to fight. But the festivities often included more informal occasions for veterans to tell their stories. This might take place over the meal that often accompanied the meeting, or as part of the ceremony itself. Many orators, explaining their decision to skip over the history of the war, as was typical, referred to this common experience. As Hooper Cumming noted in 1824, "You have often listened to the war-worn veteran, who in tears of grateful memory, recounted the alternate triumphs and defeats of those memorable times."[37]

The veterans also had a prominent symbolic role. In the morality play that most orators put on, pitting the best instincts of the United States against the forces pushing it toward decline, the veterans represented the good. They were men of "noble hearts," about whom there was nothing to say but good. The individual local veterans occupied a place analogous to the more general one that George Washington held in these orations. Even in the 1790s, when he was still president, Washington was the subject of unabashed and nearly endless mythmaking by orators. He was a "grand and good man," as one orator described him, filled with all the "virtues" one could desire.[38]

Though almost invariably short on specifics, celebrations of veterans and of Washington in particular gave the orators and their listeners an object of pure admiration to hold up. This golden object served as a mirror or counterpoint to all that was improper, undesirable, or broken in the Republic. Using veterans as objects of admiration was particularly effective for the orators because it sidestepped the difficult problem of how to celebrate American unity while criticizing one's present-day political enemies. Because the veterans' relevant actions and virtues lay in the past and were acknowledged by all present, they were in a sense beyond reproach. (A contrary approach, using for instance then-President Thomas Jefferson as the exemplar of the "perfect man," as one orator did in 1803, could leave a far more partisan taste in the audience's mouth.)[39]

The veterans present at the assemblies added substance to the thin abstraction that the republic was under threat and required its citizens to defend it. In an 1803 address to the inhabitants of Dighton, Massachusetts, David A. Leonard stressed the need to protect the "national freedom" of the United States from the "enemy without the walls" who continued to threaten it. Speaking directly to the Revolutionary War veterans in the crowd, he exhorted them to be prepared to "repel an invading foe." "Our dependence for external protection is upon you," he assured them.[40]

Yet already in the 1790s, veterans of the war were becoming scarcer at Fourth of July celebrations. Lifetimes in the eighteenth century were far shorter than they are today. A man who was forty when the Peace of Paris was signed in 1783 would have already reached the average lifespan for the era, the mid-fifties, by the late 1790s. Many certainly remained: Even famous revolutionaries such as John Adams and Thomas Jefferson survived into the 1820s. But orators at the turn of the nineteenth century already spoke of veterans in language that left no doubt about their increasingly decrepit appearance to the public. One orator, elaborating on the prospect of an invasion of the US territory, imagined that if this should happen, the "ghosts of our aged forefathers shall arise" to fight again.[41]

The language used regarding the veterans emphasized their growing physical frailty, which mirrored the fragility of the Republic whose moral center they exemplified. Hooper Cumming evoked the "hoary heads" of the few remaining veterans in 1821. Andrew Dunlap, a young lawyer and future leader of the Jacksonian Democrats in Massachusetts, used a bit more imagination when he conjured the veterans who had already "descended to the tomb." Of those who "survive," he added, most had already "retire[d] from the honors and the bustle of life." Gad Hitchcock, a veteran by then in his eighties, dilated on the passage of the war generation in an 1829 oration: "Those worthies . . . are now nearly all mouldering in dust. But few remain, and those trembling on the furthest verge of life." Solomon Lincoln Jr., who was himself just twenty-two years old when he took to the podium, used his 1826 oration to call on Congress to fund pensions for the "few" remaining veterans.[42]

The rapid geographic expansion of the United States after the end of the war played a role in the thinning of veterans' presence at some celebrations. Expansion exerted a powerful attractive force on older communities, drawing away those who hoped to improve their economic situations by leaving their homes. The young were the most likely to participate in this kind of financially motivated mobility. But veterans, especially those who were members of the lower class or were indigent, were also commonly in motion. The long-settled regions of New England, such as coastal Massachusetts and Connecticut, which had some of the highest percentages of veterans, were among the most likely to experience out-migration.[43]

The passing of the revolutionary veterans meant losing the direct narrative connection to the moment of independence. In the public imagination, it also signaled a potentially dangerous weakening of the nation. If, as David Leonard asserted, the presence of the veterans was reassuring as a bulwark against invasion, their absence created a source of danger. The danger could be construed as physical: The veterans would not be there to defend the territory in the event of an invasion. This was precisely what John Holmes suggested in an 1815 oration reflecting on the War of 1812. "The heroes of the revolution were gone, the art of war was forgotten." The country needed new "officers and soldiers," but "we had none who knew how to create them."[44] But for most, their role on the Fourth was more rhetorical. Their absence would be felt first and foremost as a sign of moral danger, not as a weakening of the nation's military defenses.

Orators took the opportunity of the earlier generation's passing to exhort their audiences to meet the standard of patriotism they had supposedly established. The lawyer and historian David Ramsay, in an address filled with allusions to the passing of the revolutionary generation, expressed confidence that the "love of country has descended from father to child." Others linked the generational shift to a broader transformation in American politics. Nathaniel Bowen was explicit in his 1803 oration that the country was undergoing a moment of transition. In earlier phases of the revolution, Americans had embraced "passions" and a "high indulgence in revolutionary feelings." Now, he argued, at the "present" moment, the Republic needed "stability, not change." Like many of his compatriots, Bowen worried that this might also be the start of a decline. "Already the animosities of party sour social intercourse. . . . Already we behold a relaxation of zeal for the public good. . . . Already . . ." He went on for some time in this catastrophizing vein.[45] With the republic a mere twenty-five years old, he feared it might already be coming to an end.

The Fourth of July during the last decade of the eighteenth century and the first decades of the nineteenth century was an occasion for celebration, for triumph—even for Americans to engage in a bit of self-congratulation. Revelers did not stint in their praise of the United States.

But the resounding cheers were accompanied by far more somber notes. As they reflected on the security of the Republic, the fate of similar countries and revolutions, and the inexorable passage of time, orators on the Fourth painted a picture of the American Republic as a fragile and perhaps evanescent presence. There was no particularly encouraging precedent or model abroad for the survival of the kind of untried "experiment" that Americans had undertaken. The revolutionary veterans, who gathered the authority of the struggle for independence around themselves like a halo of safety, were a dwindling band in the early nineteenth century.

For orators during these first decades, in short, the Republic seemed to be constantly in danger of degradation or dissolution. This dark and foreboding idea occupied a prominent place in the panoramas of the Revolution that the Fourth conjured into being every year.

It was only as the American "experiment" passed its fortieth birthday in 1816 that orators began to grow more confident about the fate of the Republic. Buoyed by the recent US victories in the War of 1812, they for the first time dared to hope that the "success of the experiment" might truly be assured.[46] Yet it was not until well into the fifth decade of the Republic's existence, around 1820, that orators finally set aside their worries about the enemies threatening the Republic from outside and turned their gaze on the dangers within.

Detail of *Anti-Slavery Picnic at Weymouth Landing, Massachusetts*, ca. 1845, by Susan Torrey Merritt. Mixed media on paper. Courtesy of the Art Institute of Chicago.

CHAPTER 3

ENEMIES WITHIN

July 4, 1832: The flags waved, the cannon roared, and for the fifty-sixth anniversary of the Declaration of Independence, James Humphrey Wilder stepped forward to give an oration to the "Young Men" of Hingham, Massachusetts.

The family Wilder belonged to had been settled for nearly two centuries in the small town southeast of Boston. James Humphrey had recently graduated from Harvard, where he had been a member of a debating society. He would go on to author a handful of poems and other discourses.[1] The winning combination of local belonging and a fine education was probably the reason the committee of "Young Men" had invited him to speak to them that year.

Wilder's theme, a familiar one to his listeners, was the mortal danger threatening the nation. He was especially worried about internal divisions that tore at the fabric of the "republican system." "We have more to fear from ourselves," he warned, "than from any foreign foes." The greatest danger came from those who wanted to "divide" society into "classes . . . between high and low, rich and poor, the learned and the unlearned." These were not idle worries: The United States had been buffeted by major social and economic changes over the previous two decades, which had created and deepened social divisions. To keep the Republic intact, he exhorted his listeners to shoulder an exhaustive and eclectic list of civic "duties," from voting in elections to avoiding the "moral slavery" of fashionable clothing.[2]

The young man was in good company focusing on the dangers that the United States faced from within. Starting in the mid-1820s, orators turned their critical gaze inward. James Knowles, in an 1828 speech entitled "Perils and safeguards of American liberty," drummed out a litany of internal "dangers" that the United States faced, among them the "distinction[s]" of wealth, "ambitious" office-seekers, and misinformation spread by the free press. Unchecked, he predicted, these ills would cause the Republic's "precipitate and fatal fall." Orators became increasingly categorical in the 1830s and 1840s about the principal perils arising from within the nation. "It is ourselves whom we have reason to fear," sententiously intoned Boston's town orator in 1844.[3]

Though orators agreed that the Republic was endangered from within, they split into two camps regarding what the danger was and how to respond to it. Orators like Wilder, who belonged to the white property-holding classes, viewed social conflicts primarily as a threat to the unity of the nation. Many of them believed that individual choices and behaviors, rather than economic and social forces, were the causes of the conflicts in American society. This individualized view of the dangers the nation faced colored every aspect of their analysis. They recast the Revolution in a moralistic vein, viewing it as a struggle within men's souls as much as a fight for political independence. As Wilder had, with his call for citizens to do their "duties," many believed that personal moral, religious, or civic efforts would best address the dangers from within.

Another cohort of orators during these years took a very different tack in thinking about the nation's inner enemies. Starting in the 1820s, organizers of some celebrations began inviting orators from groups that had not been heard from before on the Fourth. They included Black men, women, members of the working classes, and members of religious minority groups. These orators shared the belief that American experiment was endangered from within, but they saw the threat in more collective and social terms. They denounced growing economic inequality, the power of capital, the perpetuation and solidification of racial and religious hierarchies, and the subordination of women. Orators in this camp told the story of the Revolution as a struggle to achieve rights and equality. They called on their listeners insistently to complete this unfinished revolutionary project. The competition between these versions of the long revolution became increasingly fierce during the 1830s and 1840s. And beneath them a third story was emerging, one that would eventually consume both: the Revolution as a struggle over slavery.

Americans' turn inward took place against the backdrop of significant economic and social changes, both in the country itself and in the larger transatlantic world.

The French Revolutionary and Napoleonic Wars, which raged with only brief interruptions from 1793 to 1815, were an economic boon to the United States. US produce, including wood and tar for building ships as well as grain needed to feed armies, found ready markets in the Atlantic world's wartime economy. Because the United States remained neutral in the conflict—or at least tried to do so—American shippers took control of a growing share of the carrying trade, transporting goods across and around the Atlantic. On land during this period, changes began slowly but surely. The first factories appeared in New England; the South experienced a land rush and an explosion in cotton production.[4]

During the two decades after the wars ended, the United States entered a phase of rapid economic development. In the South, plantation agriculture powered by the labor of enslaved people expanded dramatically while industrialization took off in the North. Driving and fueling both kinds of economic takeoff was a transportation revolution, initially centered around the construction of canals, which sped up the movement of people and goods. Economic growth brought social change, as industrialization reshaped labor relations and families in the North and the racial composition and hierarchy of the South. It also spurred heated political debate about the role the government should play in channeling and encouraging economic development. There were bitter disagreements about the use of tariffs to protect industries, the creation of "internal improvements" (infrastructure), and control of the banking system. Policy toward Native Americans and their land was another area of deep division. Then in the 1840s, a massive wave of migration from Ireland and elsewhere in Northern Europe brought rapid, controversial demographic change to the nation's cities.

Movements of religious revival and moral reform exploded onto the scene during the 1820s in response to these changes. New England, Upstate New York, and the upper Midwest were these movements' heartland. The reform movements ranged from modest efforts to improve the lives of working people to radical-feminist organizing. Religious revivals took a variety of forms. Existing Christian churches expanded dramatically, preaching a new doctrine of salvation that was more accessible to a wide public. The religious fervor gave rise to a number of new Christian faiths, the most famous and enduring of which are the Shakers, a celibate sect known for their communal living and carpentry, and the Church of Jesus Christ of Latter-day Saints (colloquially called Mormons), which is today one of the world's fastest-growing religions.[5]

Seen from the distance of centuries, it is easy to say that many of the changes that took place from the 1820s through the 1840s made the United States more powerful and secure. Economic growth, improved transportation, and population growth all helped to ensure that the United States became one of the world's great powers by the end of the nineteenth century. Reform eventually improved the lives of many Americans. Yet for those who were living through them, the transformations were a source of conflict and anxiety. New economic and social relationships had to be negotiated. Old certainties were falling away faster than they could be rebuilt. What was rising in its place could seem objectionable, if not downright wicked. As Americans looked in the mirror on the Fourth, trying to understand the present and future of their Republic, many saw a worrisome prospect.

For the traditional sort of Fourth of July orator, men such as James Humphrey Wilder, the turbulent decades from 1820 to 1850 called for reimagining the Revolution as an individualistic process: a "moral struggle," as one dubbed it.[6]

The Boston orator Peleg Chandler offered a remarkably unsparing vision of what an individualized politics would look like in his 1844 oration. Chandler claimed that the individual was the essential, and indeed the only, unit of the social world. There was no distinction between individuals and states for him: A state was merely an "assemblage of individuals." Collective "self-government," the heart of the American revolutionary achievement, was made possible by "self-government by each individual." In order for republican government to succeed, it was necessary that citizens "bring themselves under the restraint implied" by the notion of self-governance.[7]

Chandler extended this vision of the Revolution into a broader rejection of *any* kind of collective behavior or action. He regarded all organizations as suspect and warned his audience against becoming too identified with any group: "Let no man merge his identity in the masses." This admonition went for "moral associations" (roughly equivalent to what we would call nonprofits) as well as for the "business world." He was especially critical of "corporations," which tended to "diminish the feeling of personal responsibility" that was necessary for success in business. Chandler was an equal-opportunity individualist, just as adamantly opposed to collective behavior in private affairs as he was to the action of collectives in government and politics.[8]

The idea that "self-government by each individual" was the only path to protecting the Republic resonated faintly with the old Machiavellian discourse of virtue—but with key differences. Like their eighteenth-century predecessors, the mid-nineteenth-century orators saw the cultivation of interior qualities, of virtue, as essential to the continued existence of the state, which was constantly threatened by collapse. A handful of orators explicitly invoked the eighteenth-century language. William Fondey, in 1838, recalled the "lessons of antiquity" and reminded his listeners that "the spirit of freedom has never deserted the republic, until the people have deserted themselves." Yet orators in the 1830s and 1840s had a more expansive view than their eighteenth-century forebears regarding who could cultivate virtue and thus help the Republic endure. The writer Edward Everett put it well in his 1835 oration: Evoking the prospect of an "enlightened people," which included workingmen as well as the elite, he and others imagined virtue as within the reach of most American men, even if not the entire population.[9]

The Revolution as an individual struggle took on a religious coloration for many Americans starting in the 1820s. Already during the years of the Revolutionary War, political leaders had framed the Revolution and American independence as providential, the result of God's favor and perhaps even an intervention in the course of history. Yet this language had not been dominant in Fourth of July orations. After 1820, orators began to speak in more explicitly Christian terms and provide increasingly elaborate religious accounts of the founding era. Nathaniel Bouton, describing the Constitutional Convention to his listeners, imagined that religion had "mingled" in their minds with political aims as they wrote the nation's frame of government. John Cross Smith, in an address titled "The Religion and Patriotism of '76," argued that religious faith had been central to the patriotism of the founding generation and ensured the stability of the political regime they constructed. George S. Wilson described Martin Luther, one of the founders of Protestantism, as the "master spirit of revolution in modern ages."[10]

Orators paired more sharply confessional accounts of the American past with passages emphasizing the important role religion had to play in the present. Charles Brickett Hadduck, speaking in 1842, began his oration with the declaration that the "real Patriot must . . . be a Christian Patriot." He went on to exhort his listeners to engage in "Another Declaration of independence" to break the fetters of moral slavery. "For this spiritual warfare," he declared, "the patriot citizen will gird himself with the whole armour of God." Another orator declared that "the extension of pure religion is . . . the best means of securing the liberty of our country." The enthusiasm for mixing religion into politics could become awkward. Ezra Stiles Ely devoted his 1827 oration to the "duty of Christian freemen to elect Christian rulers." He called for the formation of a "Christian party in politics" that would elect "good Christians" to office. Aware that this sounded suspiciously like a call for sectarian politics or unconstitutional religious tests for office, Ely protested that he wanted nothing of the sort. He merely wanted, he said, Christians of all stripes to stand together in the political arena.[11]

Some orators were much more specific about the religious failings they perceived as threatening the Republic—and the reforms that were needed to sustain it. Alexander Brown suggested that the spread of "atheism" and "infidelity" among the population was undermining the religious foundations of the American government. He did not worry so much about such beliefs among "philosopher[s]," he admitted. But when these types of beliefs spread among the "mass of society," they threatened the shared religious sentiment that he believed held the nation together. Americans had to recommit to their religion in order to secure their "civil liberty," he instructed his listeners. Dutch Reformed pastor George Bethune pointed to the prevalence of "Sabbath breaking (even in high places)." He urged the "Christian patriots" among his listeners to make every effort to spread "pure religion" as the "best mean [*sic*] of securing the liberty of our country."[12]

A large group of Fourth of July orators during the second quarter of the century identified alcohol and heavy drinking as the greatest internal dangers to the Republic—and demanded what Samuel J. May called a "Second Revolution" to vanquish them. The 1820s were the heyday of the first US temperance movement. Begun in the 1810s in response to an apparent increase in hard drinking during the early years of the century, the anti-alcohol movement became a national phenomenon. Temperance societies sprang up across the country, organizing meetings and producing a tidal wave of tracts and speeches that inveighed against drink and drunkenness. The Fourth of July became a popular occasion on which to denounce the terrible "intestine foe" of alcoholism that threatened the Republic with destruction.[13]

Temperance-inclined Fourth of July orators individualized the revolutionary struggle, much as Chandler had done, transforming it into an inner conflict. Nathaniel Tucker Bent, speaking in 1842 in little Raynham, Massachusetts, struck the usual notes of alarm about the fate of the Republic—"the return of this day excites much anxious fear"—and declared that "national virtue" was the only guarantor of the Republic's survival. As he spoke, it became clear that the virtue he imagined was not collective but personal. The worst of the nation's "vices" was intemperance. (He illustrated the point with a series of vivid anecdotes about intoxicated college students. Evidently, some things never change.) Only by banishing this evil through personal commitments to abstinence from alcohol, he argued, could the republic hope to survive.[14]

Heman Humphrey, a minister and temperance advocate active in Western Massachusetts, went the furthest in individualizing the revolution in an 1828 oration titled "Parallel between intemperance and the slave trade." Humphrey's speech, which must have lasted nearly two hours when delivered, insistently argued that intemperance was the greatest "evil" in the United States. He believed that intemperance posed a dire threat to the nation's "free institutions": "An intemperate people," he explained succinctly, "cannot long remain free." Point by point, Humphrey compared intemperance to slavery, arguing that drinking was the "worse evil." What made drinking so awful, in his view, was that it was (unlike slavery) a matter of choice: His decision to drink crushed the drunkard with "shame" and "guilt." Like those who followed him in the cause, Humphrey called for political and social action against alcohol and drinking. Most of all, though, he called for those who were drinkers to abandon their "sin" and reform their ways. Moral and political redemption would both come in good measure through individual repentance.[15]

Though Humphrey's oration was an extreme example of the genre, many Fourth of July orators in the 1820s, 1830s, and 1840s recast the revolutionary conflict in personal or even individual terms. Tinged with religious overtones, these orators told stories of the Revolution in which the struggle was not between North Americans and the British Empire. The real Revolution, which was still incomplete, had pitted Americans against their own personal vices and failings.

★ ★ ★

Competing with the individualistic stories of the Revolution after 1820 was another group of narratives that identified the Revolution with social conflict, past and present. Some members of the traditional corps of orators adopted this set of stories as their own. But it was a new crop of speakers, drawn from groups who had not previously been heard on the Fourth, who articulated these narratives most powerfully. These orators recast the Revolution as a social struggle, which had pitted groups of Americans against one another in a fight for equality. They used this vision of the Revolution to denounce the failures of American society in their day and called on their listeners to carry on the revolutionary struggle and fulfill its aims.

During the first fifty years after US independence, communities had reliably selected local notables to speak on the Fourth. The vast majority had been white men, many in early middle age. Even those chosen as orators at a younger age tended to be men who were on their way to becoming prominent local figures. These orators, in spite of their narrow social origins, imagined themselves as speaking for the populace as a whole. This was one of the reasons that orators often addressed the women in the crowds, symbolically including them in the national community they were conjuring. Yet the actual profile of the corps of orators had not expanded much at all during that half century.[16]

Starting in the 1820s and accelerating in the 1830s and 1840s, other voices began to pierce through on the Fourth.

Workingmen sponsored their own Fourth of July celebrations as early as the 1810s. The pace accelerated in the 1820s and 1830s, as industrialization took hold in much of the North and workingmen's associations grew more vocal, coming to define themselves as a separate class with their own interests.[17] Black Americans delivered more orations, and their speeches came into print in greater numbers. Initially, most of the Black Americans who delivered orations were members of the long-standing free Black communities in the North. In the 1840s and 1850s, fugitives from slavery—building on their increasingly prominent role in abolitionist meetings—became a more significant presence. Religious dissenters also began to speak up publicly on the Fourth.

New voices emerged gradually, alongside the more traditional ones, as a look at two sample years reveals. Of thirteen orations published in 1818, at least eight were by locally prominent men: officials, lawyers, and ministers. Of the twenty-eight published sixteen years later, in 1834, some twenty-one were by men belonging to these same groups. No Black orators appeared among the authors of published orations in either year. Yet beneath these apparent continuities, subtle shifts were taking place. At most one of 1818's thirteen orations was delivered by someone of modest origins: Hooper Cumming, who spoke in Schoharie, New York, may have been a well-off mechanic. The group that spoke in 1834 was considerably more varied in their affiliations. Two of the speeches published that year were delivered by independent intellectuals of modest origins. A third orator, John Morin Scott, though born into a comfortable life, made his career as a populist and was closely identified with labor politics. Two of the orators spoke at celebrations organized by specific groups: antislavery activists and a small business fraternity. At least five of the twenty-eight speakers from 1834, in other words, represented or came from groups that had not had a voice sixteen years earlier.[18]

The rising class of "outsider" orators, along with some members of the older cohort, stressed the social dimensions of the ongoing American Revolution. They viewed the trouble with the nation as collective, not individual. Rooted in deep social problems, these challenges could be addressed only by a collective embrace of the Revolution's principles. In 1829 alone, three prominent orators invoked the specter of social division: the feminist and birth control activist Frances Wright, the writer William Emmons, and the abolitionist leader William Lloyd Garrison.

William Emmons, the most traditional of the three orators, chose as his theme the effects of industrialization in England and the United States. His discourse denounced new laws on debt, arguing that they harmed the workingman. He called on his listeners to "resist [them], even unto DEATH." In a remarkable invocation of the French Revolution in Francophobic Boston, he asked his listeners rhetorically if they would not find it "glorious" to stage a revolt like the Parisians in 1789 and "fall at the walls of our American Bastille in Leveret street"—a notorious Boston jail.[19]

William Lloyd Garrison's antislavery address, also delivered in Boston, picked up the old thread of the jeremiad. Garrison, who would soon become one of the leading voices of American abolitionism, the editor of a key journal, *The Liberator*, spoke to his audience with lacerating directness. "Our politics are rotten to the core," he averred. The worst danger to the nation, the "gangrene preying upon our vitals," was the institution of slavery. He painted a vivid and grim picture of the suffering of the enslaved, urging his listeners to see them as fellow human beings. But he was much less interested in "analyz[ing] the horrors of slavery" than in insisting that Northerners reckon with their implication in slavery. All of those in the region, he insisted, "are constitutionally involved in the guilt of slavery." Northerners were "shackled by unjust Constitutional provisions" to their Southern slaveholding brethren.[20] Was this an invocation of division or a dark vision of unity? It was, in a sense, both. Garrison knew the North and South had different relationships to the institution of slavery; in this sense, he was calling out division. Yet he also insisted on the tight bond that the Constitution established between the two sections.

Frances Wright, speaking in Philadelphia on the same day as Garrison, stated flatly that "the revolution we this day commemorate [is] incomplete and insufficient." Gesturing at a copy of the Declaration of Independence placed on the table next to her, she added that its promises of freedom and equality were "not yet" fulfilled. (An excerpt is on pp. 202–205.) She perceived multiple failings in the American body politic that were hindering the Revolution's full accomplishment. She denounced the limitations of public education and called for the creation of a "system . . . of republican instruction." This would help the people become "enlightened," thereby improving the quality of government. Wright also denounced broader social problems that she perceived in the United States. The "accumulating evils of neglect, poverty, vice, starvation, and disease" were "crush[ing]" ordinary Americans. She urged Americans to "distribute the wealth we accumulate" more widely for the "benefit" of all.[21]

Like many of the other new voices that began to speak out on the Fourth during these years, Wright emphasized the self-critical purpose of the orators and their orations. Her role, she bluntly explained, was not to "flatter" her listeners or to praise them. She had what she called the "more honest, the more useful, but the . . . more thankless task" of offering "words of counsel, or, if it must be, of reproof." On its face, this charge was not so different from the one that decades of orators had willingly assumed. Yet the critical notes would certainly have resonated with a different intonation if delivered in a woman's voice. And in denouncing inequalities of wealth and social misery, Wright and other orators of the 1830s and beyond stressed a different kind of revolutionary failure: not merely a moral or intellectual shortfall, but the very real and concrete limitations of the American project. "Liberty and equality" were proclaimed as an "abstract truth," Wright explained, but it remained for them to be "practically secured."[22]

Members of the labor movement also established a growing presence on the Fourth. In 1836, the organizer Seth Luther took the rostrum to denounce the "deception" to which workingmen had been subjected. They were constantly told that the United States was a free country and that they controlled it. But "workingmen, have been most grossly, wickedly, and most abominably deceived." The "real governor" of the United States, its real ruler, was not the people but "a spirit of monopolizing avarice, cold, heartless, unfeeling, insatiable avarice." Workingmen had to unite with one another and complete the work of the revolution, which the founding generation had only "commenced." Just as the "workingmen of 76 stood on our battle field," so "we of 36 despise the power of domestic foes." William P. Briggs, a minor official in Vermont, had foreshadowed the substance of Luther's speech a few years earlier, denouncing the "pride and extravagance" that he believed had displaced the healthy subsistence economy of the Republic's early years.[23]

The best measure of the spread and impact of prolabor orations was that they excited a strong countercurrent. In 1835, George Washington Bethune was at pains to denounce "strikes" and efforts to "array the rich and poor . . . against each other." His argument was a forceful callback to the notion of the Fourth as a parenthesis of solidarity in a country divided against itself. He asserted that under a "free government" all the parts of the body politic had their "interests . . . so intimately combined" that "an injury to the one is of necessity an injury to the other." "We are one," he declared, and he urged his listeners to reject any attempt to create "distinctions" within. A similar sentiment, rejecting any kind of division of society into classes, was expressed by Samuel Goodrich.[24]

Samuel Osgood, in his 1839 oration dedicated to "Mechanics and Manufacturers of Nashua," New Hampshire, tried to be both prolabor and proharmony. A minister and the son of a Revolutionary War veteran, Osgood hoped to head off any "prejudices" or disagreements on the Fourth. Like many other orators, he worried about the "internal dangers" and divisions that threatened to destroy American "liberties." So he tried to reconcile the warring groups by arguing that their interests were in fact convergent. The "working classes," he asserted, "are the true conservatives of our country": all they wanted, he said, was "equal laws, a free field, and fair play." Then addressing the professionals and the property owners, he urged them to "respect" the mechanics. For "you are all useful . . . and depend upon each other." Yet even Osgood himself did not seem entirely convinced. A few minutes after this ringing exhortation to harmony, he was back to mulling over the "interesting question" of whether the Republic was headed for a "speedy ruin."[25]

From a different perspective, though no less energetically than the labor orators and their opponents during these years, members of the Church of Jesus Christ of Latter-day Saints lay claim to the orator's bully pulpit. The LDS Church had come into existence around 1830, after a New Yorker named Joseph Smith declared that he had received a series of divine revelations. The Church grew rapidly, in spite of facing vicious discrimination and violence, and its adherents were soon moving west in an attempt to find a place where they could practice their faith freely. By the late 1830s, the LDS faithful had found their way to Missouri and were preparing to continue their journey farther westward.[26]

In an address delivered in 1838, one of the church's leaders, Sidney Rigdon, denounced the failures of the American experiment in the starkest terms. There was "no country," he charged, that so fully revealed the "depravity of the human heart." Hatred of the Latter-day Saints was so strong that it overcame even the formal protections for freedom of worship provided by the Constitution. Rigdon insisted, however, that the Declaration vindicated the Saints' right to worship as they saw fit. He went so far as to argue that the protections for religious liberty in the United States extended even to "Pagan[s]"—a remarkably capacious argument for the era. He concluded with a stirring appropriation of the Declaration, declaring that the Latter-day Saints "proclaim our liberty on this day, as did our fathers" and like them pledged "our fortunes, our lives, and our sacred honors" in the defense of their faith.[27]

Over the two decades after 1830, the inward-facing social critique of the United States leveled on the Fourth by outsiders both strengthened and broadened. A growing number of orators took up their banner, denouncing monied interests and forms of hereditary privilege. Edward Bangs had already in 1823 warned his audience to "watch . . . against the intrusion of aristocracy," by which he meant "the aristocracy of wealth or of birth." In South Boston twelve years later, J. V. C. Smith took up the same theme, this time acknowledging that the divisions Bangs had hoped to avoid were very real. American society was divided between "the rich and the poor." Yet he managed to maintain a measure of optimism. In his view, the two parts of the community were "mutually dependent" on each other, unlike in Europe. So long as this mutual dependence remained in place, "no lasting evils can arise from a monied aristocracy" in the United States.[28]

The screed against inequality delivered in 1836 by Orestes Brownson, a poet and member of the Transcendentalist movement, gives some idea of the reach of the outsiders' critique. Brownson had in common with Seth Luther his relatively humble origins. He also shared the belief, voiced by so many of the outsider orators, that the promises of the Declaration—and of the Revolution more generally—were far from accomplished. "Our mission is only begun," he told his listeners near the crux of his speech, nearly sixty years after the Declaration's resonant words had been publicly proclaimed. For him, as for Luther and others, entrenched social inequality had become the most durable and obdurate obstacle to achieving the Declaration's promise. He decried the inequality among "classes" in the United States, fiercely denouncing the fact that some lived in "luxury and idleness" while others would "starve" if they did not work. Work in this society became not a route to dignity but a means of "riveting . . . chains" on the lower classes. Political leaders were to blame as well: "Legislators seem not aware that there are such creatures as workingmen in existence, except in the penal part of their legislation." Instead, he denounced, they worked only for the benefit of "capitalists, landholders, stockholders."[29]

The fearsome tone of Brownson's attacks on privilege, unlike Luther's, was not matched by an equally radical program for continuing the Revolution. Luther called on his listeners to mobilize for combat against the wealthy, the "monopolists," and their political agents. The suggestion was that present-day actors had a quasi-military duty to engage in a revolutionary war, a war of independence, against the holders of privilege. Brownson did not see the need for such radical and direct action. The remedy he proposed was gentler: instituting "republican education" throughout the country. In a significant gesture for the 1830s, he urged that it be extended to girls as well as boys.

The goal of this "education" would be to train American children to "see things valued according to their worth—not in the market—but in themselves." Over time, this training would presumably ensure that Americans would avoid the harmful pursuit of wealth and would turn away from their—in his view—excessive subservience to the holders of capital.[30]

Though new voices were the most aggressive in leveling a social critique of the ongoing American Revolution, they were not the only ones. A number of individuals who fit the traditional profile of an orator—white, male, middle-aged—took part in the social reinvention of the Revolution during the 1830s and 1840s. This group of orators, like Brownson, was particularly taken with the idea that education was the key to the success of the ongoing Revolution. James B. Shepard, speaking at a celebration in Raleigh, North Carolina, presented public enlightenment as the only way to "preserve" the achievements of the Revolution. He urged his listeners to think about whether they had "provided for American literature" and done enough to "encourage American genius." Creating "seminaries of learning, to improve the heart and cultivate the intellect," he argued, was crucial to the prospects of the United States enduring as a political project. For Levi Hubbell, a prominent New York state official, spreading "useful knowledge" among the population was the only way to protect liberty in what he called "revolutionized America."[31]

In his lengthy oration delivered in 1842 in Boston, the educator Horace Mann made a powerful case for education as the essence of the ongoing Revolution and the only way to secure its survival. Mann painted a dark picture of an American Republic then nearing its seventieth birthday. He compared Americans to "Xerxes and his plundering invaders," then delivered a well-reasoned and rather devastating critique of the American constitutional system. It was "the most complex government on earth," one which demanded extreme levels of deftness and virtue to operate successfully. Because it was a government into which the popular will "entered" at every point, it depended for its proper functioning on the "intelligence" and good behavior of the populace. As a result, potentially "fatal" dangers hung over the Republic: the "danger of ignorance" and the "danger of vice" among the people.[32]

The solution to these ills was the education of young Americans. Mann did not call for reforms to the political system, legislation on public morals, or even changes to the party system (though he did critique the ferocity of party sentiment). "Complain of President or Congress as much as we will," he observed, but so long as they are elected by the populace, the complaints must be directed to the people at large. "If the country is an active volcano of ignorance and guilt, why should not Congress be a crater for the outgushing of its lava?" What was needed to fix the nation's societal and political ills, Mann argued, was the "improvement" of young minds. It was by attending to the education of "the child whose voice first lisps to-day" that Americans would be able to ensure the future of the Republic. The project of sustaining the revolutionary Republic would thus be enacted through a project of education, an inner process that would spread a form of "enlightenment."[33]

Like most others of his class, Horace Mann did not articulate a critique of American society grounded in the recognition of inequality and discrimination. His conception of the nation's ills was more moral and intellectual than grounded in material differences. Yet even though Mann did not show much awareness of the economic inequality that ran through the speeches of Wright and Garrison and Luther, the story he told about the nation's ills and how to solve them was closer to the outsiders' collective vision of the Revolution than the stark individualism of Peleg Chandler and his ilk.

The inward gaze that spread through Fourth of July festivities starting in the 1820s was a response to the nation's newfound security, but it became a means to expose even deeper and more frightening dangers.

The revolutionary American Republic's successes on the international stage were what spurred the turn inward in the first place. What had been, in 1800, a new, small, and rather unsteady state had become, by 1825, an economic powerhouse with a rapidly growing population settled on an expansive territory. Fears of invasion or manipulation by European powers, in this context, seemed increasingly remote. For orators, whose eyes were fixed on diagnosing the ills of the Republic, this sense of external security merely meant that the danger must be coming from within. Orators searched, whether in their troubled psyches or in the era's smoldering social and economic conflicts, for the enemy that threatened the nation from the inside.

Americans who listened to Fourth of July orations during the 1820s and 1830s heard a message that was at once dark and tentatively hopeful. Speakers like Heman Humphrey and Peleg Chandler called on Americans to reform their individual beliefs and behaviors. They promised their listeners that if they could do it—not so very much, really!—the salvation of the Republic would be assured. For the Seth Luthers and Frances Wrights, the nation's situation was more serious and the task ahead more arduous. Powerful interests and deep-rooted prejudices had entwined their tendrils throughout the body politic. They would have to be overcome if Americans were to save the Republic from destruction. The path they offered was longer, but they all saw a way to fix what was broken by completing the Revolution.

Yet as they trained themselves to look inward, the orators' eyes landed more and more often on a subject that resisted all solutions: American slavery. Slavery, as would become increasingly clear during the 1840s and 1850s, was an "intestine foe," an enemy within, that could not be excised without cutting into the flesh of the Revolution itself.

36 FOURTH OF JULY.

FOURTH OF JULY.

—— Men like household goods or servile beasts,
Are bought and sold, kidnapped and pirated;
Driven in droves e'en by the Capitol;
Then haul our striped and starry banner down;
Our cannon freight not; stop the noisy breath
Of heartless patriotism; be our praise unsung.
To-day we'll not discourse of British wrong,
Of valorous feats in arms by freemen bold,
Nor spit on kings, nor tauntingly call names;
But we will fall upon our bended knees,
And weep in bitterness of heart, and pray
Our God to save us from his gathering wrath;
We will no longer multiply our boasts
Of Liberty, till *All* are truly free.

W. L. Garrison.

Final page of the *American Anti-Slavery Almanac* for 1844, including a poem by abolitionist leader and Fourth of July orator William Lloyd Garrison. Courtesy of the New York Public Library.

CHAPTER 4

SLAVERY

July 1852 brought the usual wave of celebrations on the Fourth. The banners floated, the trumpets sounded, and orators strode up to podiums across the country to deliver their speeches. Of the hundreds of orations delivered that year, thirty-eight were published as pamphlets—more than usual, but hardly a record.

Slavery was a dominant theme of the Fourth in this seventy-sixth year of American independence. The immediate cause of orators' focus on slavery was the so-called Compromise of 1850, a group of laws Congress had passed two years earlier in an attempt to settle the nation's long-standing divisions over slavery. The most controversial provision of this contested compromise was the Fugitive Slave Act, which empowered enslavers to use the US federal courts to pursue people who had fled slavery and commanded the cooperation of Northern courts and police in the hunt for fugitives. By nationalizing slavery's reach, the legislation tore at the divisions that had long existed among Northerners regarding how to respond to their complicity in the institution of slavery. The law and its effects became a subject of vigorous debate in the North, on the Fourth of July as on other days.[1]

Slavery's rise as a major topic for Fourth of July orations, however, had already been underway for more than two decades before 1852. The stage had been set starting in the 1820s by orators' inward turn, which led them to focus on the dangers that faced the Republic from within. Orators in this mode could hardly avoid landing on the subject of slavery, which was an obvious and obviously dangerous source of division within the nation. Even orators who were not opposed to slavery per se—and there were many—were drawn to the subject of slavery because of the way it troubled national unity. Slavery sat squarely at the intersection of the local and the national, posing difficult questions about the cohesion of the American union and the completeness of the Revolution. The growing number of non-elite and non-white men who delivered orations after 1820 were particularly attracted to the subject: As a system of unfree labor and a form of racial caste, slavery embodied two of the main social ills that this camp of orators saw as their duty to denounce.

During the 1830s and 1840s, radical abolitionists seized upon the Fourth as a prime occasion to prosecute their argument against slavery. The radical abolitionist movement, composed of several competing streams, advocated for the immediate and complete elimination of slavery, which it characterized as a grievous moral and political crime. Abolitionist orators developed a distinctive, powerful rhetoric on the Fourth of July from the tradition's building blocks. They narrated the American Revolution as an antislavery political movement. Embracing wholeheartedly the idea that the Revolution was still in progress, they used this version of the American founding to fiercely assail the institution of slavery as it existed in their days in the United States. Fusing approaches from both groups of orators in the 1820s, they urged their listeners to both examine their own consciences and engage in a wider social struggle against injustice.

The most famous Fourth of July oration of the nineteenth century, Frederick Douglass's 1852 speech delivered in Rochester, New York, is a masterpiece of this tradition. Often examined in isolation, as a solo rhetorical tour de force, Douglass's speech was in dialogue not only with other abolitionist speeches but also with the broader practice of Fourth of July oratory. By remolding old tropes about the ongoing Revolution and the multiple geographies of the revolutionary struggle, Douglass succeeded, in a way few others had, in throwing into sharp relief the incompatibility of slavery with American revolutionary ideals, and the vital need for his listeners to join in the struggle against it.

Slavery had already emerged during the 1820s as a prominent theme in how Americans thought about the Revolution. This was true not only for radical abolitionists and their equally fierce opponents but also for citizens across the political spectrum. Slavery's moral weight and its ubiquity in the national conversation played a role in its growing presence on the Fourth. But orators also dwelled on the institution of slavery because it raised questions about the connection between local and national politics and the ongoing character of the Revolution that had fascinated Americans on the Fourth for decades.

The growing interest in slavery among a broad cross section of orators can be seen, albeit imperfectly, by tracking the appearance of the word *slave* in orations over time. Mentions of slavery increased tenfold over the sixty years between 1780 and 1840. Before 1800, in a sample of 190 orations, "slave" appears in only 12 (6 percent of the total). In a sample of 578 orations published between 1801 and 1820, "slave" appears in 88, some 15 percent. (Even within this period, the usage accelerated considerably from one decade to the next: 55 of those appearances were in pamphlets published after 1810, for 21 percent of those orations.) After 1820, the numbers exploded. Out of a sample of 484 orations published between 1821 and 1840, "slave" appeared in 311 of them, or 64 percent.[2]

One reason for slavery's growing ubiquity on the Fourth was that it threw into stark relief the contradictions in the federal structure of the American Republic, challenging orators to rethink the geography of the Revolution and the nation. Slavery had been a part of the social order in North America since the earliest days of European settlement—in New England as well as in the Southern or middle colonies. Over the course of the eighteenth century, leading up to the American Revolution, the regions began to diverge, with slavery expanding rapidly in the southern half of the future country and holding steady or even retreating in the North. By the 1790s, slavery was already well established as one of the hallmarks of division between the country's regions, serving as a durable dividing line within the shared political space.[3]

As abolitionism gained ground in the North during the first decades of the nineteenth century, orators on the Fourth stressed slavery's regional character. A Black orator, the carpenter William Hamilton, underscored this division in his 1827 speech delivered in New York City the day after slavery had been legally abolished in the state of New York. After giving his discourse a conventional opening, which framed the abolition of slavery as a triumph for the "principles of liberty" set forth in the Declaration of Independence, he took a sharp local turn. He insisted that any mention of Washington and Jefferson in these speeches had to be accompanied by citation of an alternative pantheon of abolitionists, which prominently featured New Yorkers, including John Jay and Alexander McDougall, leading figures in the Revolution in New York. He concluded his speech by offering "best thanks and wishes to the State of New York" for abolishing slavery within its borders.[4] The invocation of general "principles of liberty" had thus narrowed into a distinctly regional phenomenon by the end of the speech. Revolutionary liberty, far from being national, was finding its fulfillment at the level of the individual state.

The deepening division etched by slavery in the geography of the United States complicated the quintessential Fourth of July exercise of rhetorically uniting the nation and setting it apart from others. Orators struggled to transition from the local to the national, as was their wont. This was the problem that Elisha Bartlett faced in his 1848 speech in Lowell, Massachusetts. He began by recalling his early life in Lowell and describing the community as one that set aside its differences. He then swept to the national level, lauding the "fundamental structure and principles" of the US government, and describing it as "alone amidst the nations of the earth." He then devoted many minutes to making invidious comparisons with Europe. Yet even as he painted the picture of unity and strength, he was forced to acknowledge "one contradiction"—the presence of slavery in "some of the states of the Union." This division loomed larger as he continued, leading him to worry aloud, in his last minutes on stage, about the "dissolution of the Union" and the "disruption of the bond" that united the states.[5]

More threatening still was the way slavery tied parts of the United States more firmly to foreign places than to its own states. Comparisons between the United States and other places in the world had consistently been one of the main arrows in orators' rhetorical quiver. Some of these comparisons had been far-fetched or very approximate. It was clearly a stretch to assert that the American presidency was similar to the Ottoman sultanate, or that the social structures of the United States were comparable to those of France or the Netherlands, although this did not stop orators from attempting to make such comparisons.[6] It was, on the other hand, easy to see similarities between slavery regimes foreign and domestic. Slavery was the product of an international trade that had been underway for centuries, characterized by similarities in legal structures and racial prejudice worldwide.

When orators considered slavery from a comparative perspective, as they often did while surveying the United States, it sowed doubts about the superiority of the American project. Elisha Bartlett admitted that the "contradiction" of slavery in the US was "greater and more flagrant, than any I have attributed to England." The same worry caused Charles Train to concede that the presence of slavery meant that "France is not the only nation on earth inconsistent with herself." The fact of slavery's existence, by disturbing a central pillar of the national story that orators were creating on the Fourth, became an itch they could hardly avoid scratching. Some tried to avoid it anyway. Nelson Mitchell, giving an oration in Charleston, South Carolina, in the late 1840s, made elaborate comparisons between the US and Europe, especially France, but studiously avoided a whisper about slavery.[7]

Orators' habit of looking for comparisons abroad made the Fourth a congenial occasion to argue for "colonization" as a solution to the problem of slavery in the United States. The American Colonization Society, founded in 1816, sought to resolve the slavery question by sending the Black population of the United States (both those born free and emancipated enslaved people) to Africa or another destination abroad. Though colonization was vehemently opposed by Black activists, it had a significant following among white Americans over several decades. Giles Bacon Kellogg, in an address to the antislavery society of Williams College, from which he was then graduating, denounced the "evil of slavery" and assured his listeners that colonization was the only viable solution. The colonizationist plan, he said, leaning on language that was very familiar to his listeners, was an "experiment" that they had to undertake. A few years later, when Yale professor Benjamin Silliman declaimed against the "enormous evil" of slavery, he also argued that the only way to lift this "sin" from the "national conscience" was to emancipate slaves and send them to Africa.[8]

In the same way that slavery warped orators' geography, it challenged speakers on the Fourth to think about the critical question of whether and how the revolution was still ongoing. Augustus Woodbury, speaking in Lowell, Massachusetts, in 1855, took the position that slavery "denies" the "very opening sentence of the Declaration of Independence." To fulfill the promise of the Declaration, the eradication of slavery was required. In the ongoing struggle that orators imagined between the forces of creation and destruction, slavery was one of the forces destroying American liberty: "The breath of the slave destroys the constitution of your liberties," argued one orator. The struggle against slavery was the culmination of the struggles that had defined the Revolution. So long as slavery existed, the Revolution was incomplete. Charles Wentworth Upham called in 1842 for the "final triumph of human rights over every vestige of feudalism, and every form of slavery," within the United States. This "final triumph" would mark the accomplishment of the revolutionary project.[9]

The opposite position—that slavery was an integral part of American society and that to threaten it was to threaten the Revolution—was also well represented in Fourth of July rhetoric in the 1840s and 1850s. Joshua G. Wright, orating in North Carolina in 1851, described abolitionism in the plainest terms as an attempt to undo the "political association" formed in 1789. In short, abolitionism was, in his view, an *anti*-revolutionary movement. And this was not the case only in the Deep South, where such rhetoric might be most expected. Robert Stockton, speaking the same year in Elizabethtown, New Jersey, argued firmly against abolitionism, equating it with a new kind of political oppression. "At the South," he declared, in response to this new form of tyranny, "the watch-fires of the revolution have been rekindled in the preparation for the defence of their homes and firesides." He asserted, in case the point was not sufficiently clear already, that efforts to abolish slavery had "no warrant in the Constitution."[10]

Nowhere was slavery more vividly present at mid-century than in the orations delivered by members of the rising abolitionist movement. Abolitionism experienced a significant transformation during the 1820s and 1830s. Its roots stretch back to the eighteenth century, when enslaved people and small groups of white humanitarians began to systematically question the regime of Atlantic slavery. Initially, much of the opposition from white people focused on the horrors of the transatlantic slave trade. This movement achieved tangible victories starting in the 1790s, and in 1807 both Britain and the United States enacted bans on the trade. In parallel, enslaved people attacked the institution of slavery. They had their greatest success in Saint-Domingue/Haiti, overthrowing the slave regime during the 1790s. But enslaved people also achieved a number of local and temporary successes both within and beyond the United States during this period, including significant limits on slavery in Massachusetts, major revolts in the American South and northern South America, and the short-lived abolition of slavery in the French Empire.[11]

Political movements against slavery coalesced in the United States and elsewhere in the Atlantic world during the 1810s and 1820s. These ranged from associations that sought to ameliorate the condition of enslaved people to groups calling for the total, unconditional abolition of slavery. In the United States, divisions emerged in the 1820s between proponents of gradual and immediate abolition. The so-called immediatists demanded that slavery be abolished at once, without compensation for the enslavers. The larger group of "gradualists" proposed a variety of mechanisms to gradually abolish slavery, ranging from "free womb" laws (which freed children born to enslaved women) to schemes for compensated abolition that stretched over years or decades. By the early 1830s, the hostility between these two camps of abolitionists in the US had become nearly as fierce as any disagreement between them and the defenders of slavery.[12]

For American abolitionists, the Revolution was a conundrum, an ambiguous reference point that could be used to ground the righteousness of the abolitionist cause or to undermine it. On the one hand, the era's foundational documents—above all the Declaration of Independence—articulated universal principles that could be readily used to challenge the institution of slavery. On the other side of the balance sheet sat the ugly fact that many of the founders of the nation—including all of the early presidents from Virginia—held people in bondage. The US Constitution encapsulated the seemingly irreducible tension surrounding slavery in the American founding era. The Constitution did not use the word "slave," and was silent on the general legitimacy of slavery. It contained a provision allowing the abolition of the slave trade after twenty years. Yet the notorious three-fifths clause, which counted enslaved people as a fraction of a free person for the purposes of determining representation, legitimized and even rewarded slaveholding.[13]

There was nothing obvious about the radical abolitionists' wielding of the Revolution's principles against the present day. Indeed, for many of them it was difficult to attack slavery precisely because it had clearly been a well-established institution during the era of the American founding. Minister and abolitionist leader Adin Ballou made clear just how tricky a needle this was to thread. After beginning his 1843 speech with a denunciation of the Constitution for its compromises with the slavery regime, Ballou asked rhetorically whether it was not disloyal to his "patriot ancestors" to attack the Constitution. He concluded that it was not, since he was only obliged to praise and honor his forebears insofar as they were guided by "truth and righteousness." "Must I hallow their errors" or "worship their weakness," he asked his listeners. Of course not, came the reply.[14]

Radical abolitionists settled on a simple yet powerful rhetorical strategy on the Fourth: They identified what they believed to be the antislavery principles of the Revolution and flagellated the United States for failing to live up to them. They read the Declaration of Independence as a forceful affirmation of the "equal natural rights of man." Orators in previous decades had by no means ignored the discussion of natural rights in the Declaration, but it was the abolitionists who amplified the place of natural rights in the Declaration to the exclusion of almost everything else. This allowed them to accuse Americans of betraying the principle of natural liberty. Americans who did not demand immediate emancipation, claimed one of them, were turning "self-evident truths" into "self-evident lies." Abolitionists' distillation of the Revolution's ideals to natural rights led some to equate slavery with a rejection of the Revolution itself. Only if the "people [were to] repudiate the Declaration of Independence as a rotten and dangerous instrument" could slavery be made consonant with American ideals.[15] Failing to commit to abolition was tantamount to abandoning the Revolution.

Immediatists regarded the contradiction between the celebration of natural rights in the Declaration and the practice of slavery as not merely a failure but also a form of hypocrisy. The Reverend Joseph M. Corr, a Black Methodist minister in Philadelphia, declared in his 1834 oration that slavery was an "audacious insult" to God and a "libel" on a "republican government." He cited the language of the Declaration to urge his largely Black audience to take up their rightful place as an "equal race." William Lloyd Garrison, for his part, imagined what would happen if he were to "stand up before a European assembly" to talk about the United States and "[denounce] the usurpations of a kingly government." It would be impossible for him to do so, because the United States was an even more desperate form of "tyranny." If he were to "make the attempt," nonetheless, to speak about the Fourth to Europeans, he went on, "the recollection of my country's barbarity and despotism would blister my lips."[16] Here was a vision of the United States as not merely similar to European powers, but not the slightest bit freer. Indeed, if we take Garrison at his word, the United States in the mid-nineteenth century was a land of tyranny that far surpassed the British tyranny that the colonists had thrown off in 1776.

As emancipation projects progressed in the Atlantic world during the 1820s and beyond, the hypocrisy of the United States became increasingly troubling. Edwin Atlee, a founding member of the American Anti-Slavery Society, speaking in Philadelphia in 1833, devoted much of his speech to demanding the "immediate" abolition of slavery. There could be no delay in the matter because "every hour is adding to the mass of our oppressed fellow beings." After making a forceful moral case for immediate abolition, Atlee observed that it was hardly unprecedented: Several other countries had abolished slavery without experiencing any "danger whatever" or any "injurious effect." Among the cases he cited were the abolition of slavery in the French Empire in 1794 and the abolition decree first issued in independent Colombia in 1821. Others would certainly have contested his assertion that these abolitions had been "peaceable."[17] Yet there could be no arguing with Atlee's larger point that emancipation was no longer an untested experiment.

Abolitionists, most forcefully the radicals and immediatists, adopted the long-standing tone of alarm regarding the fate of the Revolution and dialed the intensity up to eleven. The minister and teacher Nathaniel Prime, in a strongly antislavery oration delivered in the mid-1820s, painted a picture of a future without emancipation that was little short of catastrophic. Prime made the familiar moral arguments against slavery with fervor. But he also gave his listeners a vivid demonstration of what would happen if they continued to ignore their moral duty. After reviewing data showing that the enslaved population would continue to expand in the future, he warned that white Americans would become a minority in a large part of the country. The enslaved might then rise up and "aveng[e] all their wrongs" by killing the enslavers and taking their "lands." The example of Haiti showed that this was hardly an implausible scenario. The final sentence of his speech drove home the gravity of the situation and issued a clarion call to his audience to heed his "timely warning . . . before the sword of sleepless justice smite our souls."[18]

Like Prime, many abolitionists emphasized that although all Americans shared collective guilt for the continuation of the slave system, individuals could free themselves from this dark shadow by helping to overturn it. In 1842, one orator described slavery, in entirely conventional terms for an abolitionist, as a "stain upon the nation." Though the responsibility was collective, attached to the "nation" as a whole, the remedy was individual: "Man by man, heart by heart," they had to embrace the tenets of abolitionism. William Lloyd Garrison made the point explicitly a few years earlier. "As a people," he exclaimed, "our fingers are stained by blood." Fortunately, however, "these things are . . . not true of us, as individuals." Americans were still moral agents capable of redeeming themselves by abolishing slavery.[19]

As befits their dire warnings about the immorality of slavery and its dangers, abolitionists began to treat the Fourth as an antiholiday: a day to denounce the persistence of slavery. The most visible manifestation of this tendency was the decision to hold some abolitionist commemorations of the Fourth one day later, on the fifth of July. The program of these meetings followed the same general pattern as the traditional celebrations, featuring speeches, prayers, and sometimes a meal. (Their tone, not surprisingly, was more somber than that of a typical celebration of the Fourth.) The practice of celebrating the fifth of July had a double resonance. It underscored the fact that abolitionist commemorations focused on slavery in the United States, rather than on the state of the nation more generally. Meeting on the fifth also recalled the long-standing practice of delaying Fourth of July celebrations until the following day when the fourth fell on a Sunday, out of respect for the Sabbath. This had been done since the very earliest days of the Republic. Delaying the festivities of the national holiday allowed both days to be observed in a suitable manner. The abolitionists, by shifting the holiday in the same way, seemed to suggest that they were separating the sacred from the profane. For the abolitionists, it was the fifth that was sacred and the fourth that became utterly profane.[20]

Some abolitionists chose to move their meetings to other dates altogether, allowing for an exclusive focus on slavery and its abolition. Black abolitionists at mid-century shifted their attention to August 1, the anniversary of the emancipation of the enslaved population in the British West Indies. These celebrations, like those on the fifth, were patterned after the traditional Fourth of July, often featuring orations.[21] The creation of an entirely new holiday parallel to the Fourth, exclusively to reflect on slavery, marked a logical culmination of slavery's growing importance as a subject of reflection in American political life in the middle of the nineteenth century.

Of all the orations that constituted the rising tide of arguments about slavery, the most celebrated was delivered in

1852 in Rochester, New York, by perhaps the best-known figure of the abolitionist movement: Frederick Douglass. Born into slavery in Maryland around 1817, Douglass educated himself, against the law, and then effected a daring escape from slavery in 1838, disguised as a sailor. His rapid rise as an abolitionist speaker and activist began shortly after he arrived in New Bedford, Massachusetts, that year. His *Autobiography*, first published in 1845, was a sensation in abolitionist circles and placed him in the first rank of the movement's formidable troop of speakers and activists.[22]

Douglass's oration, delivered on the fifth of July at the invitation of the "Rochester Anti-Slavery Sewing Society," was a powerful performance by any measure. (An excerpt is on pp. 206–210.) Its reputation is justly immense, and has only grown in recent years as scholars have grappled with the depth and richness of Black intellectual life in the antebellum US.[23] Yet Douglass's oration, for all its inventiveness, was not entirely unprecedented in either its arguments or its rhetorical strategies, nor did it come into being in a vacuum. Reading Douglass's oration alongside the other thirty-odd published orations delivered that year gives a clearer sense of what was truly original in Douglass's.

For the first twenty minutes or so of his oration, Douglass's listeners would have heard little that would surprise them. After the usual disclaimers about his abilities, he passed along the well-worn grooves of the genre. He evoked the Revolutionary War, extolled the founders of the Republic, and made unremarkable comparisons between present-day politics and the founding era. The audiences that heard Thomas Starr King speak in Boston or Charles Adam Smith in Easton, Pennsylvania, that same year, got much the same speech, albeit with the usual local variations and individual flourishes.[24]

At about the twenty-minute mark, Douglass's discourse settled firmly into the grooves of the jeremiad, denouncing Americans as hypocrites and sinners for tolerating the presence of slavery. This in itself was not uncommon. There was a long tradition, as we have already seen, of orators using these occasions to fiercely denounce the errors of US politics and the failings of American society. Nor was Douglass alone in denouncing slavery in the starkest terms. Charles Adam Smith included an extensive critique of slavery. The orator that year in Lawrence, Massachusetts, also declared slavery to be a "sin" and expounded on how enslaved persons felt on the Fourth: "The air which we breathe so generous and so free begets in their heart the palpitation of fear; the soil on which we tread is like burning coals to their feet."[25]

Douglass nonetheless diverged sharply from the model of the Fourth of July jeremiad by rhetorically stepping outside of the national community. Douglass had used the second person sparingly during the first minutes of the oration, referring to "the birthday of your National Independence, and of your political freedom." But for the most part, during the conventional beginning of the oration, he had included himself among the members of the nation, calling his listeners his "fellow-citizens" on more than one occasion. This was the usual setup for a jeremiad, which was a harsh critique but one that was understood as coming from within. So it must have been a shock when Douglass abruptly set the enslaved apart from the other members of the nation: "What, to the American slave, is your 4th of July?" he asked his listeners. With a thumping repetition of the word *your* nine times in less than a minute, he stressed that the slave was not part of the nation that they were ostensibly there to celebrate. The second person also implied that he, Douglass, positioned himself on the side of the enslaved rather than among the ranks of his listeners.[26]

Douglass's excision of himself and the enslaved from the national community was a startling move. It was customary for orators to speak about groups who were not, or were not yet, part of the nation: new immigrants, free people of color, Native Americans, even members of opposing political parties. Many abolitionist orators had spoken of the enslaved before, condemning a nation that excluded so many of its inhabitants from the circle of citizenship. (Even free Black Americans had good reasons to view themselves as outsiders; they knew that many of their fellow citizens continued to regard them as at best partial members of the national community.) Yet most orators, when they pointed out the excluded, still did so as spokesmen for the people present—for free individuals who considered themselves part of the national community. Indeed, the heart of the orator's task was to forge links between the individuals standing before him and before the many far-off, simultaneous gatherings, and the imagined collective. As the orator that year in Hagerstown, Maryland, put it, "our nation is a unit." Douglass, by excluding himself from the community, seemed to be making a radical departure from this tradition of cohesion.[27]

Yet even the seemingly extreme decision that Douglass made in this passage, to exclude himself from the nation, was not as unprecedented as it appears at first blush. In the decades before Douglass delivered his speech, many of the growing number of orators who were members of racial minorities or immigrants or workingmen had taken a more combative approach to the Fourth. They saw their role, rather than papering over the divisions within the country, as unveiling its flaws to make them evident for all to see. Douglass's decision to make himself one of the excluded certainly represented a significant sharpening and hardening of this tradition. But it was discernably a part of this already robust oratorical tradition, rather than an entirely unexpected departure.

Having set himself on the side of the oppressed, Douglass offered an extraordinarily fierce denunciation of the churches that supported slavery. He excoriated the ministers who dared to mount a defense of slavery, and the Fugitive Slave Act in particular. These churches, he declared, had made themselves not merely complicit in slavery but were the "bulwark of American slavery." Their acts were a kind of "horrid blasphemy." And in case these churches had somehow missed the message, he made it explicit for them—in all caps, in the printed edition—"YOUR HANDS ARE FULL OF BLOOD."[28]

Douglass's upbraiding of proslavery ministers and churches frontally was, on the face of it, a continuation of his powerful rhetoric of self-exclusion. The church was widely regarded as above politics, and as a powerful source of national coherence. To attack it thus could be seen as a form of self-separation from the national community. But, as his audience knew well, ministers very often delivered orations on the Fourth of July. As orators on the Fourth, they spoke not exactly as men of God, but as leading members of the community. And more than a few of them, in previous decades, had used the occasion provided by the Fourth to defend slavery or at least to reject abolitionist arguments and tactics. Just the day before Douglass took the stage, in the city of Albany not two hundred and fifty miles east of Rochester, the Reverend I. N. Wyckoff had sternly warned his congregation against opposition to the Fugitive Slave Act: It was a "foul crime," he said, to "resist" even an unjust law.[29]

As he placed slavery at the heart of his interrogation of national unity, Douglass also ripped into the idea of America's uniqueness on the world stage. Drawing on the long tradition of international comparisons on the Fourth, Douglass urged his listeners to take their habitual look abroad. Many of the orators that year saw the United States, in familiar terms, as a light unto the nations, "crusade[rs] for the emancipation of mankind." Douglass and a few others that year saw something quite different when they looked abroad. "Roam through all the monarchies and despotisms of the old world, travel through South America," stormed Douglass, "and you will say with me, that for revolting barbarity and shameless hypocrisy, America reigns without rival." He inverted the traditional trope of the city on the hill, of the United States as superior to other nations. The institution of slavery could make even the most conventional orator's move on the Fourth—extolling American uniqueness on the world stage—into an occasion to recognize the profound moral failing of the American experiment.[30]

After Douglass's denunciations had reached their crescendo, he abruptly turned his listeners in a more hopeful direction. He first denounced the idea that the Constitution was a proslavery document, taking a firm stand on one of the most contested issues in nineteenth-century abolitionist politics. Then he promised to end, "where I began, with *hope*." He concluded his oration with a brief but fervid repetition of tropes that were familiar from other orations celebrating the glory of the American nation: a vision of the "fabulous Pacific," to which the United States was then expanding, and the spread of "intelligence" into the "darkest corners of the globe." (What "intelligence," exactly, he did not say.) These transformations, he wagered, would lead to the final defeat of slavery not only in the United States but also worldwide.[31]

The hopeful conclusion of Douglass's speech, like its beginning, was very much in keeping with the conventions of the Fourth of July oratorical tradition. Even the darkest, most self-flagellating oration offered some dose of optimism. Yet it was not a hollow hope that Douglass proposed here. Like many earlier orators, Douglass regarded the achievement of abolition and the final elimination of slavery in the United States as integral to the American revolutionary project. Indeed, as his friend and colleague Samuel J. May would declaim in his own oration a few years later, slavery was a "seed of evil, a root of bitterness, our fathers left in the soil, when they planted our tree of Liberty."[32] The task that Douglass charged his listeners with was to dig out that "root" and complete the work of the Revolution.

Douglass's 1852 discourse, more than most, spoke both backward and forward to the long tradition of Fourth of July oratory. Though nobody could have known it yet, Douglass's denunciations of slavery and Northern complicity would become a dominant thread in oratory on the Fourth within a decade. More and more orators in the North, mirroring their audiences' views, acknowledged the exclusion of Black men and women from civic life in the United States and found it unjustifiable.

Yet Douglass's speech, while anticipating key elements of the way the political discourse in the United States would evolve over the coming years, also marked a revival of significant themes from a much earlier era of the Fourth of

July. Though relatively few of the orators from the 1790s or the first decades of the 1800s identified slavery as a flaw in the revolutionary Republic, virtually all of them believed the Revolution to be unfinished. For Douglass, as for other radical abolitionists, it was an article of faith that the work of the Revolution was not done so long as slavery survived.

Perhaps even more striking is the way Douglass's rhetoric, and that of other antislavery orators, recalled the kaleidoscope of geographic scales that orators had used to imagine the American Revolution during the early Republic. From the 1780s to the 1820s, orators moved quite freely among the local, state, national, and international scales. It was not at all evident, to many, that the federal Republic was the main or even the ultimate container of political belonging. Many privileged forms of local belonging, or dreamed up visions of global governance. Douglass and his abolitionist peers, in their way, returned to this more capacious vision of the American nation. For them, a state or city that recognized the freedom of the enslaved—or a country like Britain that was working for it—was as much, if not more, their homeland than the United States of America as a whole.

Detail from Winslow Homer, "Fire-Works on the Night of the Fourth of July," 1868 (from *Harper's Weekly*, vol. XII, July 11, 1868). Courtesy of the Metropolitan Museum of Art, New York.

CHAPTER 5

REVOLUTION'S END

July 4, 1861: The flags waved, the cannon roared, and for the eighty-fifth anniversary of the Declaration of Independence, orators climbed the steps to their perches in the late morning to deliver their discourses. Things went a bit differently than they had even a year earlier; this was the first wartime Fourth of July in nearly a decade and a half. The previous fall, the Republican Abraham Lincoln had won the presidency. In the aftermath of the election, a large bloc of Southern states had announced that they were seceding from the United States. As the Fourth rolled around again, the union that the Declaration of Independence had created seemed to be crumbling.[1]

The Civil War and the years surrounding it profoundly changed the American Republic. The secession crisis, the war, and postwar Reconstruction reconfigured the political community, emancipated millions of enslaved people, and altered the US political system. The oratorical tradition on the Fourth of July allows us to probe how the upheavals of the Civil War interacted with the United States' ongoing revolution.

The idea of a living revolution followed a parabolic trajectory in the years from about 1855 to 1875, beginning in decline and then experiencing a sharp revival before a final collapse. During the decade prior to secession, mainstream orators asserted with growing confidence that the Revolution was finally complete. The independence of the United States was assured, and the era of political transformation was over. (Only abolitionists dissented strongly from this consensus.) Audiences in the 1850s heard a growing distance from the revolutionary era.

The outbreak of the war in 1860 led to a rapid reversal of fortunes, as orators collapsed the present into the past. Taking a leaf from some of the earliest orations, these speakers once again imagined themselves as actors in the American Revolution. This emerging sense of the immanence of the revolutionary past had several surprising effects. It forced Unionist orators to try to explain how the independence of the United States had differed from the secession of the Southern states. This problem became a preoccupation of Northern orators during the war years.

Once the war was over, the fusion that orators had effected between the past and present contributed to a general collapse of interest in the Fourth of July. Along with the rise of other commemorative celebrations, such as the holiday that would become Memorial Day, the ending of the war seemed to mark the conclusion, once again, of the revolutionary experience. Yet Black orators did not share this sense of an ending. Faithful to the pre–Civil War oratorical tradition and certainly motivated by the ongoing discrimination and struggles Black Americans faced, they continued to evoke for their listeners a living revolution in which they were active participants.

To a person who had listened closely to July Fourth orations, the scission of the Union could hardly have come as a surprise. In terms ranging from the dire to the merely offhand, orators had been warning about it virtually since the Republic was formed. In the years leading up to 1860, these warnings only increased. An "explosion" could occur and completely destroy the edifice of the US government, cautioned one speaker. Another spoke of the present moment as "the era of our national crisis" and charged Americans with "taking . . . other gods" in place of the true deity, Union. Some, like the conservative gadfly and literary entrepreneur Charles Edward Pickett (cousin to future Confederate General George Pickett), contemplated the idea of disunion with a certain satisfaction. The union of the "northern and southern sections was, from the start, a great mistake," he declared. It was an "unholy" union; the sooner it ended, the better.[2]

One way that orators expressed this anxiety—in the ever-returning circular time of the revolutionary commemoration—was to imagine a growing gap separating their present from the revolutionary past. The Mexican War had marked an initial turn in this direction. Joshua Henshaw, speaking in Utica in 1848, exulted that the recent US victory in that war had "dispelled" the doubts that had long hung over the United States' durability. The anxiety that had suffused Fourth of July oratory about whether the "experiment" of the United States government could last seemed to be finally laid to rest. Henshaw went so far as to declare the US a model that could be followed by other nations as Europe was consumed that year by a new round of political revolutions. William Greenough, giving the venerable Boston oration in 1849, proclaimed the United States the "Conquering Republic" and traced its "progress" in the Americas and what he considered its "failure" in Europe. He read the hoary notion of a fragile American Republic backward, pinning the label on Europe instead.[3]

Samuel Law's curiously old-fashioned oration, delivered in 1858 in Stamford, New York, suggested how wide the gap had grown between the present and the past for some orators. He offered a detailed recounting of the historical events of the Revolutionary War, something that had not been common in July Fourth oratory. Samuel J. May, speaking near Chautauqua two years earlier, marked the distance in a more direct manner: The "great experiment begun by our fathers in 1776 is a failure," he stated flatly. Turning the tried-and-true trope of "experiment" on its head, identifying it as a failure rather than a success, May closed the door on the continuity with the revolutionary past that orators had long claimed.[4]

An elaborate send-up of Fourth of July orations, published under a pseudonym in 1859 in Greenfield, Massachusetts, encapsulated the critical and ironic distance that at least some members of the elite felt from the Fourth and its oratory. The fake "Address," attributed to a fictional "General Herr von Louis Kershoot," was written by someone who had made a careful study of the form. Though it followed the conventions of the address to a tee, it was written as though spoken by someone with a broad rural accent: Spelling was largely phonetic, with dropped *g*'s throughout, and a casual, slang-filled vocabulary. The author knew well and poked fun at the typical flaws of orations: overly complex language ("this circumrevolutionizin' age"), bombast (compared to Washington, "Cesar becomes nobody, and Napoleon . . . is no-whar"), and long recitations of military deeds ("This fetches us smack dab into the fantasmagoria of the Mexican war!"). The oration even closed with a snide misquote from Jefferson.[5]

In the culminating part of the pseudo-oration, the author set his skeptical sights on the idea that there was a close connection between past and present. After invoking the surviving revolutionaries ("there ain' more'n about one hundred and fifty on 'em livin'"), he picked up the old thread of similarity. "The sperit which animated them, animates also, and quickens the pulse of every trew patriot." So you "have met, with the stamp of genius on your brows, to commune with the fathers and fight your battles over agin."[6] Reduced to its bare bones, and rendered in a colloquial and accented language, the sentiment of a close connection between the listeners and their "fathers" was reduced to absolute absurdity. Instead of carrying the combat of the Revolution forward—a noble calling—the listeners would "fight your battles over agin." This turned it into a mere repetition, devoid of meaning. The Revolution, in this telling, was a distant memory; the effort to bring it into the present was not only fruitless but also ridiculous.

The beginning of combat in the Civil War rebounded forcefully on the Fourth. The crisis had been gathering speed for more than half a year before the Fourth of July came around in 1861. Abraham Lincoln's election to the presidency, brought about exclusively by the Electoral College votes of "free" states, took place in November 1860. The following month, South Carolina became the first state to secede from the Union and began to refuse the resupply of Fort Sumter, a federal bastion established on a sandbar in Charleston

Harbor. Over the next six months, ten other states quit the Union and joined the Confederate States of America, created in January 1861. In April, after the newly inaugurated President Lincoln ordered that Sumter be supplied in spite of South Carolina's threats, the first shots of the war were fired, turning away the US government ships that were coming to the fortress's aid.[7]

Some of the first Fourth of July orations after the war began seemed to suggest that the idea of completeness that had reigned in prewar orations might persist. A wave of declamations that the American "experiment" had failed followed the start of combat. "We have seen the world startled by the question new and strange," declared John R. Warner in 1861: "Can the American Republic be a failure in governmental experiment?" There was of course nothing new about this question; Americans and Europeans had been posing it since the 1780s. But Warner's surprise was not entirely misplaced, given the view some had advanced in the decade before the Civil War that the republic had finally succeeded and that the experiment had thus come to a quiet and happy conclusion. George Ticknor Curtis, delivering the Boston oration, was also skeptical about the experiment's outcome, saying that many now believed that the "Union . . . has become an exploded experiment."[8]

Any persistence of the rhetorical reflexes of the 1850s was washed away, however, by a rediscovered sense of the immediacy of the Revolution. The war encouraged orators to reconnect the Revolution directly with the present. "We come together under circumstances that seem to make us *contemporaries and co-actors* as it were, with our fathers of the revolution," argued the abolitionist lawyer John Jay in 1861. The spine of his oration was a sequence of weighty comparisons between the conditions of the 1770s and the 1860s. Warner, too, invoked the idea of a close connection between the present and the past. He asserted that the "long slumbering spirit of '76 has been quickened again to life" by the war. Indeed, he went on, he considered that the war had already given the current generation an "experimental" knowledge of American "principles and pledge[s]"—through the experience of defending them in arms—that they had "never" expected to have.[9]

The bridge across time that John Jay posited in his orations was owed as much to the speaker himself as to the words he spoke. Jay hardly needed to make any explicit statement to convey his point about the connection between present and past: He was the grandson and namesake of another John Jay, the prominent diplomat, politician, and jurist of the founding generation, best known today as a coauthor of the Federalist Papers. Jay's presence on the rostrum in 1861 was a kind of incarnation of the founding generation in the present moment. This ceremonial embodiment of the revolutionary past harkened back to the presence of veterans at the orations in the first decades after the Revolutionary War, veterans who had been such a critical part of the scene setting for those much earlier celebrations of the Fourth.

As the war dragged on, putting the lie to Northern fantasies of a rapid conquest of the South, many orators found it useful to talk about the War of Independence. A number used it to evoke a sense of closeness with the past. For Walter Clarke, independence and the Civil War were twin processes: One had created "Liberty," and the other was the final stage of a struggle to "achieve loyalty also, completing the fabric which the fathers commenced." Though he considered the Civil War to be a kind of "second nativity" for the nation, in actuality it was the completion of a "task to which the American People were sent, eighty-six years ago." The two eras, in his view, existed in a state of full continuity. (An excerpt is on pp. 211–212.) Thomas Russell, in 1864, went to great pains to detail the parallels between the events of the American Revolution and those of the Civil War, finding in the earlier events close foreshadowing of the present. Speaking of 1775, he pronounced, "Here, again, we match the lesson of the past." His vision was of a kind of simultaneity of patriotism between the participants in the two wars, which closed the gap in time between past and present.[10]

Brainerd Kellogg offered what may have been the most concise and dramatic expression of the notion of closing the gap between revolutionary past and revolutionary present. In his 1866 oration, he asserted that the Fourth now stood "in the American calendar and heart as signalizing two matchless events, twin in nature, though parted by eighty-nine years of space." It represents both "the first and second births of the nation, a birth into life and a birth into liberty, a birth of generation and a birth of regeneration."[11] Kellogg's natal metaphors went in two distinct directions. On one hand, he distinguished between a "first and second birth" of the nation, suggesting what would eventually become the conventional idea of Reconstruction as a "second revolution." Yet these births were not spaced out chronologically: In spite of the years elapsed, they were "twin in nature." His vision was thus of the two events as existing—at least imaginatively—in a moment of simultaneity.

The rhetorical fusion of the present and past brought with it enthusiastic reassertions of the old belief in the ongoing nature of the American Revolution. In an oration delivered in 1864 in Yankton, Dakota Territory, the surveyor G. D. Hill presented the Civil War in stark terms as the conclusion of the American Revolution. The "fathers of the Constitution" had made a "fatal error" in allowing slavery to endure, contrary as it was to the "great fundamental principle of equality, which is the foundation of this Republic." They had done so because the new states were "weak; exhausted" and they prioritized forming a union over "strangl[ing]" slavery "as they should have done." As slavery expanded in the first half of the nineteenth century, it had left the revolutionary work incomplete. The war had now come to conclude the matter. Hill expressed confidence that slavery would "cease with the war," and that this would make a "realization of the . . . hope . . . of human rights" that had been promised by the founding generation.[12]

One of the major themes of Fourth of July orations during the war was the effort to distinguish between the Confederate decision to revolt and the thirteen colonies' Declaration of Independence. In essence, the question they posed was about the definition of revolution and what distinguished it from other forms of revolt. This had been a topic of only intermittent interest on the Fourth of July in the previous seven and a half decades. During periods of revolutionary upheaval in Europe—the 1790s and early nineteenth century, and again around 1848—a handful of orators touched on the question. But it had never merited close attention until now.

The question of how to define revolution was suddenly one of burning importance to Northern orators in the wake of secession. Southerners were making their own efforts to close the gap between the revolutionary past and the present on their own terms and claim the mantle of inheritors of the Revolution. On December 24, 1860, South Carolina state leaders issued a "Declaration of the Immediate Causes" that led them to secede from the Union. This document presented itself as a kind of anti–Declaration of Independence, reprising some of the wording of the original Declaration while flipping it on its head. It declared that South Carolina was exiting the Union and "resum[ing] her separate and equal place among nations." This rhetorical echoing of the revolutionary era had a narrative parallel. The heart of this new Declaration claimed that the acts of the American patriots of the 1760s and 1770s and the actions of Southerners during the 1850s were similar. Both were fighting tyrannical governments that had become "destructive" of the purposes for which governments were created. The South Carolinians presented themselves and the other slave states as engaged in a struggle to continue and fulfill the American revolutionaries' fight.[13]

Even skeptical Northerners had to admit that there was potentially something to this line of argument. John Jay, in 1861, was already inquiring whether the Confederates could invoke the "right of revolution." While no American could "deny" the existence of such a right, he asserted, the rebellion was no revolution. It was merely, as his title announced, a "Great Conspiracy." The writer Edward Everett, speaking in New York City in 1861, observed that Southerners were claiming to "exercise . . . the great and ultimate right of revolution." "No one" in the United States could "den[y]" the existence of such a right, since the country would not be independent without it. John Jay, firm abolitionist that he was, nonetheless admitted freely that "no American can deny" the "right of revolution." So long as the "causes of justification are sufficient," Americans had to acknowledge that it was legitimate to undertake a revolution.[14]

Unionist orators, having conceded the right to revolution, nevertheless sought firmly to distinguish between the Revolution of the 1770s and the Southern secession of the 1860s. This was more easily said than done. Augustus Woodbury, speaking in 1862, spent nearly a quarter of his oration wrestling with the problem. He began by differentiating between "revolution" and "insurrection": though some of the manifestations of the two phenomena might be similar, such as warfare and the overthrow of governments, he argued that the former was a rightful "last resort" of a people to regain their liberties while the latter was a "mad and passionate" reaction to immediate pressures. With this distinction, Woodbury appeared to suggest that there was a clear difference in kind between the American Revolution and secession. Yet no sooner had Woodbury delineated this contrast than he muddled it by conceding that there were both "preserving" and "destroying" revolutions. Only the former were to be admired or encouraged, in his view. Yet by conceding that some forms of revolution were also undesirable, Woodbury effectively obscured the difference he had been laboring to establish.[15]

Ultimately, after some further twisting about, Woodbury settled on a characterization of the American Revolution as a struggle for "ideas," which he likened to the Northern position in the current war. He dismissed the military character of the Revolution out of hand: "The battles were scarcely more than skirmishes." On the face of it, this would seem to indicate a major difference between the Revolutionary War and the Civil War, the latter of which was nothing if not a scene of major battles. But he drew this distinction only to argue for a deeper commonality: Both wars were in his view manifestations of the "power of ideas"; each was a "struggle for great principles." Woodbury argued that over the previous decades of the nineteenth century, a struggle had been underway between the "spirit of liberty" and the "institution" and "spirit of slavery." It was this "struggle for independence" that concluded with the election of Lincoln in 1860, marking "the victory of freedom." In this narration, the Civil War was the result of a long "struggle for independence," in which the North played the role of the eighteenth-century patriots.[16]

By July 1863, the core of Unionist orators' distinction between the two moments, Revolution and secession, was not really ideological but temperamental in nature. They stressed the patience of the revolutionaries of the late eighteenth century, in contradistinction to what they saw as the unseemly, immoral, and impolitic haste of Southerners in 1860 and 1861 to escape from the Union. Thus Jordan Stokes, a Unionist orator in Nashville, Tennessee, in 1862, found that the "patience" of the founders after 1775 was what made their Revolution a legitimate one. The South in the Civil War, by contrast, had begun a "groundless revolution." Orville Hickman Browning, speaking in Quincy, Illinois, recounted the "years of suffering" that the patriots of the late eighteenth century had endured before deciding to revolt. Samuel Kirkland Lothrop, delivering the Boston oration just after the war ended, called secession "without cause" because it was not rooted in grievances that Southerners had "endured"—with the suggestion, embedded in the word itself, that long suffering was in some sense the measure of an uprising's legitimacy.[17]

Orators' decision to collapse the temporal gap between the Civil War and the Revolution—their sense that the Revolution was again immanent—proved to be both powerful and dangerous: powerful in the sense that it impressed upon the soldiers and civilians of the 1860s the urgency and transformative potential of the revolutionary generation. Yet the collapsing of time was a hazardous enterprise as well. Imagining the Civil War as part of the revolutionary era meant grappling anew with the divisions and disagreements of the Revolutionary War—and particularly with the competing interpretations of the Revolution that Southern politicians were advancing.

The surrender of the Southern armies and the end of the war in April 1865 signaled the start of a new and decisive phase in the transformation of American politics. As they had for nearly a century, Fourth of July orations provided a mirror and a space for reflection on the state of US politics and the direction it would take in coming years. Yet the postwar era also wrought a transformation in both the Fourth of July holiday itself and the orations that marked the occasion, making the discourses not merely a vehicle of change as they had been in the past but also a symptom of the larger political transformation.

The ten years from 1865 to 1875 constituted one of the most consequential eras in a nineteenth-century American political odyssey that was not short of such moments. The end of the war raised complicated questions about how to reconstitute a Union that had been broken by secession and conflict. Serious disagreements arose among the dominant Republicans, and even more so between congressional Republicans and Republican President Andrew Johnson, about how and when to readmit rebel states to the Union and how to reintegrate Southerners into the nation's political life. The question of how to approach the abolition of slavery and manage its aftermath was, if anything, even more fraught. This struggle, in addition to the passage of important civil rights legislation by Congress, spurred the adoption of constitutional amendments that fundamentally changed the contours of US citizenship and the franchise, opening both to Black Americans—albeit with significant limits in practice.[18]

A corresponding sense of rupture flowed through the post–Civil War orations. J. W. Hough, in a Fourth of July address delivered in Santa Barbara, California, in 1873, made this rupture explicit. He divided the "history" of the United States into "three great eras." The first, which ran from the earliest settlement to 1800, was the phase of independence. The second, which encompassed the antebellum decades of the nineteenth century, was one of "growth." During these two periods, "we have been contending for certain great political ideas, for the independence of the nation, for the equality of men." But now in the post–Civil War era, in this "very different period," these "old issues are dead." Now it was new questions, "prosaic but vital" ones, such as honesty in public office, that were at the center of political debate. L. H. Gulick, speaking in Honolulu just after the end of the war, declared that the "experimental period in American history is mainly past. The American system . . . is no longer a partially-tried experiment." Like Hough, he believed that this new era involved both the passing of old problems and questions as well as the need to deal with new kinds of troubles.[19]

The sense of rupture in the aftermath of the Civil War extended to doubts about the very utility of the orations themselves. The decreasing number of orations being published during these years was one sign of how communities were questioning the speeches' value and role in the national conversation. While some continued to appear in newspapers, in the form of summaries, the number of orations published in full as pamphlets dwindled rapidly in these years. During the fifteen years from 1851 to 1865, publishers had put out an average of nearly twenty-eight orations per year as pamphlets. In the decade after 1865, the number dropped to just eleven.[20]

Reconstruction-era orators worked their doubts about the orations' form and the holiday itself into their texts. B. B. French, giving an oration in Washington, DC, in 1870, simply refused to offer a "regular 4th of July oration" recounting the founding era. It would be a "tale told for the thousandth time, and to which I doubt if I could find, in all this assemblage, half a dozen attentive listeners." His critique was echoed by another in 1871, who wondered whether the speeches were now merely "hackneyed phrases." Another orator in 1870 began his speech by wondering whether the Fourth of July orations in general were "played out." He eventually came around to the idea that this was not so, but he clearly regarded it as an argument that needed to be made, rather than, like some of his predecessors, a pro forma concession.[21]

Part of the explanation for the diminishing interest in orations during the Reconstruction era had to do with the fusion of past and present that audiences and orators had embraced during the war. For a sizable portion of Americans, the struggles of the Civil War had not only become identified with the revolutionary past but had also come to actually eclipse them. Charles Francis Adams—one of the era's most celebrated documentary editors, hardly a man to ignore the past—declared in his 1869 oration that he was commemorating a "double anniversary," calling to mind two more recent early July events alongside the Declaration of Independence: the Battle of Gettysburg (July 1–3, 1863) and the capture of the fortress of Vicksburg on the Mississippi (July 4, 1863). Adams concluded from this coincidence of dates that "this celebration . . . now . . . belongs to us, as well as to our fathers."[22]

As Adams's address hinted, in the 1860s and 1870s the celebrations of the Fourth were being eclipsed by new commemorations. Through the wars and social conflicts of the nineteenth century, the Fourth had remained the foremost annual occasion to speak on the nation as a whole. The Civil War fixed a new set of dates in the calendar that served that purpose. For some, especially but not exclusively Black Americans, it was the anniversaries—for there were several—of the end of slavery. For many others, especially the hundreds of thousands of families of those who had fallen in the war, it was Decoration Day, which originated in May 1865 and would eventually become Memorial Day. Orators on the Fourth were very conscious that new commemorations were supplanting the old festivities. George B. Loring mentioned this explicitly during an 1868 Fourth of July discourse in Salem, Massachusetts, one of the cradles of the July Fourth oratorical tradition. "We meet today with new associations, new duties, new memories—a new people—to commemorate [those who] died that we might have a country." The suggestion was clear that the celebration of the Fourth had now taken on another character, with its long-standing associations now twinned with or even trumped by the "nobler" accomplishments of the Union Army.[23]

The Civil War's amoeba-like incorporation of the Revolution extended to many of the familiar tropes of the orations. One speaker in 1866 announced that he would not give a detailed account of the recent war because it was "too well known at every fireside to dwell upon it." This, of course, had been the repeated refrain of orators for decades after 1776. The 1866 orator John G. Brown hammered the point home, echoing his long-ago predecessors by gesturing to the veterans in the audience: "Around me today I behold evidences of that dreadful, yet glorious, Civil War in the wooden limbs, the empty sleeves."[24] As for orators working immediately after the Revolutionary War, the presence of veterans served to both underscore the proximity of the events and authorize the speaker to pass over the details of the war itself.

The 1870 Boston oration delivered by William Everett expertly summed up this sense of the Revolution's simultaneous immediacy and irrelevance. It was Everett who began his oration by wondering aloud whether the Fourth were not "played out." Everett gamely tried to make it timely. As orators frequently did, he accomplished this in part by trying to seize the mantle of a major anniversary. Inconveniently for him, 1870 marked only the ninety-fourth anniversary of the Declaration. However, if one numbered the Boston Massacre orations out of which the Fourth of July oration had developed—the first had been delivered in 1771—this marked the one hundredth year of orations. This rather strained effort to cloak 1870 in a larger significance suggests how much the Fourth had lost its perceived importance over the previous decade.[25]

Undaunted, Everett insisted on the living quality of the occasion. The "truths of the Declaration" were not, "as yet, worked out," he declared. They had been enunciated in 1776, but they were still in an ongoing "process of development." And the present day, the Fourth of July, was one of the moments during which that meaning would be unfurled. It was up to those who were present to make it happen. "We are not enacting a pageant" today, he insisted to his listeners, "but doing a great work"—bringing the principles of the Declaration into practice. "Like our fathers," he went on, in so doing we will "mutually pledge to each other our lives, our fortunes, and our sacred honor." The deliberate echo of the language of the Declaration of Independence cast Everett's listeners not just as participants in the struggle, but as participants equal to their ancestors.[26]

Everett did not content himself with vague platitudes about the Declaration. He offered a specific and locally tailored plan of action for how his listeners could work to bring the Declaration's promises into concrete form. This entailed solidifying the national union through the creation of a means of "communication between the extremities of the country." It also meant opening wide to the world, and not just to Europeans. For several pages, which would have lasted a few long minutes during the performance of the oration, he declared himself in favor of allowing unlimited Chinese immigration. This was not only good policy, he argued, but also a necessary way of "putting the Declaration into the freest and fullest practice." In another nod to the long tradition of orations, Everett made sure to reflect on the role of the local community in this national and global project: New England's role, he stated, would be to "perfect" the national work, not to be "pioneers."[27]

One group remained quite faithful to the pre–Civil War model: Black orators. Their loyalty to this model was largely due to their sense—which fewer and fewer white orators seemed to hold—that the Revolution remained both in progress and incomplete.

As early as July 1865, when the South had only just laid down its arms, Black orators returned to the well-established trope of the Fourth of July as an occasion for self-examination and self-criticism regarding the elements that had not yet been achieved. The Reverend E. J. Adams, a leading figure in the Black community in Charleston, South Carolina, spoke to a large crowd in one of the community's Black churches. In an initial oration, Dr. M. I. Camplin had already noted that the Declaration's "teachings" had not been "carried out in reference to our race." Adams hammered the point home. Like many Black orators before, he observed that only the "initiatory steps" had been taken toward the full extension of rights to Black Americans. Adams concluded by observing that there was ample precedent for the extension of rights to those who had not yet enjoyed them: in Europe, the "peasant" had been "descended from a slave" and had long been held in contempt. But peasants had eventually made their way to the "summit of liberty and equality"—and this history gave him confidence that Black Americans could do the same.[28]

An orator in 1868 in New Orleans offered an even more distilled version of the Black political imaginary in the wake of the Civil War. The speaker, Captain Chapman, extolled the Declaration and the War of Independence, at the end of which "the national heart rejoiced, for liberty was at last won." Yet, he swerved, "how incomplete it was" while slavery persisted and "many of God's image remained in . . . bondage." It had taken another "war of independence, shorter . . . but infinitely more destructive" to complete the abolition of slavery. Even in its wake, however, "the work is not yet complete, and we cannot afford to rest." The expansion of the right to vote remained an ongoing battle that required continued vigilance and struggle.[29]

For John G. Brown, an affiliate of the Black-serving Wilberforce University who delivered an oration in 1866, the idea of an ongoing revolution was a central theme. Brown's oration followed the conventional pattern of such addresses. He started off by recollecting the Revolution's history, briefly narrating the imperial crisis and the Revolutionary War, then turning to the postwar period. "But mark you," he warned his listeners, "the work of building a nation was not complete when victory was secured." This familiar trope, which usually introduced a discussion of the Constitution, took on a much wider ambit in his oration. "Thank God," he added, "there were men among us who believed that when the fathers declared 'all men are born free and equal,' it applied to the poor black slave." The antebellum abolitionists, such as William Lloyd Garrison and Elijah Lovejoy, had taken up the "mantle of [James] Otis," a tribune of the patriot party in Massachusetts and an early opponent of slavery.[30]

The ongoing revolution of the nineteenth century had reached its first culmination in 1859—though John G. Brown hardly regarded its course as fully run. The raid on Harper's Ferry that year by John Brown (no relation to the speaker), which gave "definite shape" to the "principle of universal liberty," awakened the nation "from its dream." The armed abolitionist stirred up the "mouldering bones of the heroes of '76" and caused "their spirits" to "ignit[e] in the breasts of the loyal men of the nation." The resulting war, the orator explained, had created "unbounded liberty" in the United States. Yet, he insisted, there are "yet dangers ahead; we have not fully attained that growth . . . that we can afford to rest from that vigilance that should characterize watchful citizens."[31] Like Chapman, and echoing the once-familiar tropes of white orators, John G. Brown viewed the work of the Revolution as an ongoing struggle.

Though it was marked by significant continuities, Fourth of July oratory by Black men after the war nonetheless took part in the general recentering of the holiday on the national level. Antebellum abolitionist orators had been among the deftest thinkers elucidating the multiple scales on which political community might be imagined. Some had used the abolition of slavery at the state level to attack the national government's complicity in the institution; others, like Frederick Douglass and Garrison, had not hesitated to praise foreign places for being further ahead in the struggle for liberty. While Reconstruction-era Black orators continued the tradition of focusing on the present and the future, they now largely embraced the framework of the nation. One of the key strands in the polyphonic vision of the American Revolution that had been present since the founding era had now come to an end. The achievement of nationwide abolition had finally made it possible for even Black orators to reflect on the Revolution's meaning primarily at the level of the United States as a whole.

The Fourth of July, which for nearly a century had been a key moment when Americans considered the shape and extent of the revolutionary project, experienced a curious fate during the Civil War and Reconstruction. The war and its aftermath made concrete and real the direst fears that had shivered through the speeches of orators on the Fourth year after year. Speakers at the rostrum had endlessly reminded their listeners of the "experimental" character and fragility of the American Republic, and had rarely shown much confidence in its durability. In 1860–1861, the long-anticipated breakup had come at last.

Over the course of the war and then in the early phases of Reconstruction, the North had undertaken an unprecedented project of nation building. Through the creation of a mass national army, the strengthening of the central government at the expense of local power, and the stimulus given to national-scale commercial and industrial enterprise, the war that had threatened to destroy the Republic ended up solidifying it beyond all expectation. In this sense, the war and its aftermath finally fulfilled the wishes of generations of orators, who had long called for greater unity and cohesion across the many fragmented units of the American nation. Union orators, Black and white, were absolutely right to see in the war and Reconstruction a fulfillment and accomplishment of political projects that had begun in the 1770s, from the making of a nation to the establishment of equal rights.

Yet, perhaps rather paradoxically, the solidification of the nation during the Civil War era was accompanied by a distinct drop-off in interest and attention accorded to the Fourth and the holiday's intellectual lodestar, the orators. With its immense traumas, the war spurred the creation of new commemorations, superseding older ones, including the Fourth. But the Fourth and the orations were not merely eclipsed by competing events of the same kind. A more fundamental transformation had occurred: The accomplishment, for the first time, of *real* nation building rendered the Fourth of July orator obsolete. A country with the fundamentally localist character of the antebellum United States had always needed intellectuals to explain and validate its coherence. Once the nation had been forged on the battlefield, that role quickly came to be seen as far less essential.

A Fourth of July orator with the thumb of "special privilege" looming over him. Udo J. Keppler, "Independence Day," from *Puck*, July 1, 1908. Courtesy of the Library of Congress, Prints and Photographs Division.

CHAPTER 6

AFTERSHOCKS

July 4, 1941: With war raging around the world, millions of radio sets in the United States tuned in to hear President Franklin Delano Roosevelt's message on the anniversary of American independence. His oration was short and straightforward. In 1776, the United States "waged war on behalf of the great principle that Government should derive its just powers from . . . representation chosen in free elections." This "cause" had since "swept the world," but it was now under threat: "The fundamentals of 1776 are being struck down abroad." Roosevelt called on Americans to stand up for the principle of free government around the world, to "save freedom" from "dictatorship." Six months later, the Japanese attack on the Pearl Harbor naval base brought the United States into the world war.[1]

By the time Roosevelt delivered his brief oration in 1941, only distant echoes of the earlier tradition of Fourth of July oratory remained. The Civil War and its aftermath had already begun to sideline the Fourth. The political transformations of the 1860s and early 1870s had stitched the states more tightly together than ever before, diminishing the need for orators to tell their unifying stories. Other celebrations of national community, which were more centered on the Civil War and its heroes, competed with the Fourth for national attention. Contemporaries in the aftermath of the Civil War were already cognizant of this change and the Fourth's dwindling importance.

The Fourth's transformation accelerated during and after the centennial of American independence in 1876. The federal government took unprecedented steps that year to establish a national narrative around the Fourth and reshape its rhetoric in a historical vein. At the heart of the transformation that took place over the next hundred years was a conviction, which had already been budding at the end of the Civil War, that the Revolution was finally and firmly complete. Orators used the occasion of the Fourth less and less to incite their listeners to continue the Revolution. They presented the completed Revolution as an exemplar to other places, to be sure, as a model for the world, but hardly as an event still in progress. Even those who adopted a critical tone in their oratory about social and political problems—such as socialist, labor-oriented, or suffragist speakers—did not look back to the American Revolution for solutions to these problems, but rather sought answers elsewhere.

In the twentieth century, orators did more than just relegate the Revolution to the past tense; they made the Fourth of July intellectually inert. The annual celebration had long been charged with intense debate about the nature and boundaries of the American political community. As Fourth of July orators themselves often observed, nineteenth-century oratory had its faults—too long, too bombastic, full of clichés—but blandness and insipidness were not among them.[2] In the hands of orators after 1900, the Fourth of July discourse increasingly became a bland recitation of platitudes. The time for debate had ended, and little remained of the Fourth but a happy, festive void, a celebration of the nation shorn of its critical edge.

Looming over the Reconstruction-era orations was the rapidly approaching one hundredth anniversary of American independence. The fact that this anniversary seemed so significant was itself a novelty. In most of the world before the nineteenth century, centennial and multi-centennial anniversaries did not have the special importance that has come to be attached to them. Annual commemorations were common—like the kermesse, a local festival connected to a church or local saint, which was widely practiced in

Northern Europe. Anniversaries of decades or fractions of a century were not uncommon for celebrating the lives or reigns of monarchs. Various religious commemorations, from millennial anniversaries of churches to jubilees every fifty years, punctuated the calendar. The centennial, as a special date, was a newer way of marking time.[3]

For the federal government, empowered in the wake of the Civil War, the centennial of the Revolution appeared to be a perfect occasion to show off the state that the war had created. The commemoration centered on plans for a massive Centennial International Exposition to be held in Philadelphia. The exposition was modeled on the Universal or International Expositions—also known as the world's fairs—which were an important part of the cultural scene during the nineteenth and early twentieth centuries. This would be the first event of its kind to be held in the United States. Like the era's other expositions, this one focused on displays of the nation's industrial and economic might, with exhibitions that showcased recent American innovations, such as the telephone and mechanical calculators. These industrial curios were mixed in with more explicit remembrances of the Revolution, including a statue of George Washington and a massive fountain, twelve feet high, which featured four nine-foot-high statutes, among their subjects such revolutionary-era figures as the founder Charles Carroll and the early naval hero John Barry.[4]

As the exposition was being planned, the federal government also intervened in the commemorations of the

Fourth across the country—and in the oratorical tradition. In March 1876, Congress passed a joint resolution urging the "several counties or towns" of the United States, when they assembled to celebrate the Fourth, to "cause to have delivered . . . an historical sketch of said county or town from its formation." They asked that copies "of said sketch . . . be filed, in print or manuscript" in the office of the county clerk and with the Library of Congress. The goal was to create a "complete record . . . of the progress of our institutions during the First Centennial of their existence." This resolution was taken up by the president and former Union general Ulysses S. Grant, and it was promoted in the form of proclamations in May and June.[5]

The Congressional resolution pointed toward a major transformation in the function of the Fourth and its oratory.[6] The resolution thrust aside the orator's traditional incitement to live as though the Revolution were taking place in the present. Congress instead called for memorial orations, "historical" in nature, that would take stock of the "First Centennial" as a discrete moment in time and create a "complete record" of it. Even though this Congress was newly empowered by the results of the war, it could not and would not have proposed such a radical transformation of the Fourth of July oration if the event had not already, during Reconstruction, lost the centrality it had long enjoyed in the US political imagination.

Along with a high degree of grassroots interest, Congress's intervention produced a huge spike in the number of published orations in 1876. Library catalogs and collections suggest that there was a roughly tenfold increase from the number of orations published in the previous year. This marked a reversal, albeit a single-year one, from the decline of orations that had taken place during the previous decade and a half, and a return to the prolific publication of orations that had been typical in the middle of the nineteenth century.[7]

With few exceptions, the published orations of 1876 followed the directives of Congress and the president. These were historical discourses that took the occasion to recount the development of the town, usually from before the earliest European settlement to the present. Henry Clay Platt, for instance, offered a long address in Huntington, New York, to which he affixed the title "Old Times in Huntington: An Historical Address." The pamphlet opened with a reprint of Grant's proclamations and delivered the promised historical account in minute detail over what must have been well over an hour.[8] The sources on which the orators drew, and the style they deployed, were notably different from earlier years. Gone were the soaring language and sweeping generalizations that had been the orator's usual fare. The 1876 orators were heavy on facts, presented in serried ranks marching steadily toward the present. "The Town of Huntington was first settled in 1653—223 years ago. The settlers were Englishmen. The Pioneers, who formed the settlement, consisted originally of Eleven families, who found their way across the Sound from Sandwich, Massachusetts":

Thus began Platt's recitation of his town's history, a typical performance.[9]

A surprise result of the historical bent of the 1876 orations was that Native peoples made a sudden and massive entry onto the Fourth of July stage. Orators over the previous century had made brief, often veiled references to Native American societies. Indeed, they had usually done no more than obliquely refer to the elimination of Native peoples. The historical turn of 1876 suddenly made Native populations a central subject. John Crowell, speaking in the town of Haverhill, Massachusetts, gave a long excursus toward the beginning of his oration about the "Indian hostilities" in the region during the seventeenth century. This portion of the address was nearly five times the length of his discussion praising the town meeting—a favorite subject of earlier New England orators. The orator in Providence, Rhode Island, spent most of his oration praising Roger Williams, the seventeenth-century founder of the colony of Rhode Island, whom he celebrated in good measure for his supposedly peaceful and benevolent engagement with local tribes.[10]

Particularly striking in this regard was the oration given by William Arny in Santa Fe, New Mexico. Arny was an antislavery figure of the prewar period, who became an Indian agent and Secretary of the New Mexico Territory during part of the Civil War. He had close connections with Native groups in the territory and took the opportunity of giving the address to bring Native peoples to center stage in the story of Santa Fe. His history of the town gave a prominent role to the Pueblo Indians as the chief antagonists of the Spanish during approximately two centuries of settlement. His language was infused with condescension and hostility toward Native American civilization and culture. Yet in comparison to the silent erasure of Native people from most earlier orations, it marked a major step toward recognition. Arny also took the opportunity to directly address the Native Americans. In an echo of the century-old practice of calling out members of the audience, he pointed out that "a number of the descendants of these Indians are before us," and saluted their "honesty and native intelligence."[11]

The emergence of the subject of Native Americans in the orations in 1876 was yet another indication, in the wake of the Civil War, that the idea of an ongoing revolution was fading away. Indigenous people were depicted by white Americans in the later nineteenth century as belonging to the past. For an orator, focusing on Native people was a way to situate himself rhetorically in a time increasingly remote from the present. At the same time, the elimination of Native peoples by the rising United States had never truly been seen as a part of the "revolutionary" project. (Whether the logic of the United States and its founding was in fact genocidal is another question; I am speaking only of how nineteenth-century authors viewed the matter.)[12] To put the elimination or disappearance of Native life in North America at the heart of an oration was incompatible, rhetorically, with the idea of the Revolution as an ongoing process.

The tradition of fiery oratory, though thoroughly submerged beneath a tsunami of historical reminiscences in 1876, was not entirely extinguished. Indeed, among advocates of women's suffrage, it got something of a boost. The women's suffrage movement had been bitterly disappointed by the failure of national leaders to include provisions for women to vote in the Reconstruction-era constitutional amendments and legislation. The national leaders of this movement—particularly the well-off white women who were among its most visible advocates and who moved in the elite circles from which Fourth of July orators were usually drawn—denounced the fact that women were still deprived of equality even as the voting rights of immigrants and Black men were being protected.[13]

Women's suffrage leaders, like Black orators during Reconstruction, proved themselves in 1876 to be among the most faithful students of the tradition of Fourth of July oratory. In a series of speeches delivered in Philadelphia on the sidelines of the centennial celebration—whose organizing committee had refused to include the suffragists—advocates of suffrage revived the idea of an ongoing revolution. Women's rights, declared Belva Lockwood, would come as part of the inevitable turning of the "wheel of the revolution": Its onward progress, in the present, would ensure that women would "inherit the liberty of which the Declaration of to-day is the chief cornerstone."[14] An article sparked by discussions of these and other speeches at the centennial led the editor of a feminist newspaper, *The Ballot Box*, to declare that a "Ladies' Revolution" and a "feminine war of independence" appeared to be imminent.[15]

The feminist orations remained faithful even to the Fourth of July oration's traditional tendency toward harsh criticism. In one particularly biting speech, the equal rights campaigner Sarah J. Spencer denounced the legal imbalance between men and women when it came to children born out of wedlock. After beginning with a pathos-ridden depiction of the travails of poor mothers whose children were under the legal control of their husbands, she observed that there "is a child a mother may own." The "men who make our laws," she observed, have made it so that "the child born out of wedlock is given by law to the mother! (Indignant applause.)." A crescendo of sarcasm followed, calling on "modest men" to come forth and claim paternity of such children: "We women will call them out and lay the crown of fatherhood upon their modest brows."[16] Here, the fierce sense that the Revolution was not over—that there remained much work to do to bring the ideals of the Declaration into practice—was alive and well.

The female orators who spoke outside the Centennial Exposition, however, were the exception rather than the rule. Most of the oratory surrounding the centenary, like the speeches delivered across the country under the federal government's direction, were essentially historical and celebratory in character. The critical spirit and sense of the immanence of the Revolution, which had both been such crucial elements of Fourth of July orations for a century, were largely absent.

In 1905, the city of Boston commemorated the Fourth, as it had each year since 1777, with its annual official oration. The town fathers invited Le Baron Colt, a distinguished senator and federal judge from nearby Rhode Island, to address them. Colt struck a triumphal note from the very first phrases. On this day, he reminded his audience, "was begun . . . the most remarkable experiment in government the world has yet witnessed." In earlier years, this usually would have introduced an extended set of worries about the fate of the United States. Instead, less than a minute later, Colt declared the experiment a complete success: "Lo! we now behold, as the *outcome* of this experiment, the fairest picture of government which ever met the eye." A few minutes later, he addressed himself directly to the "prophets of evil omen": the writers and thinkers, among them many orators from previous generations, who had predicted the imminent downfall of the American Republic. Their predictions had not come true, he said, and they never would. The Revolution was over, and it had been successful.[17]

As Colt's address suggests, the already attenuated tradition of Fourth of July oratory declined further in the decades after the centennial. The post–Civil War shift toward viewing the Revolution as finally complete solidified and became, as Colt suggested, an article of faith for orators and audiences. Simultaneously, the tradition of publishing orations declined and became more tightly focused on eminent, usually nationally recognized figures. In previous generations it had been the usual practice to call on local notables to deliver orations, but many of the individuals who spoke and whose orations were published were hardly prominent beyond a very local context. This limited decentralization now came to an end, replaced by a wholly national approach.

After 1900, virtually the only orations that were published were those delivered by US presidents and other nationally prominent figures. Theodore Roosevelt, who gave, very early in his public life, a Fourth of July address in 1886, delivered a number of orations during his presidency, many of which were published in the press. His successor, William Howard Taft, while repudiating much of Roosevelt's presidency, continued this practice. His 1911 speech at the National Home for Disabled Volunteer Soldiers was officially published by Congress. Some of Woodrow Wilson's orations were published as well, including a 1918 speech delivered on the Fourth at Mount Vernon, George Washington's plantation. The exceptions to the general truth that it was presidents' orations that were published tend rather to prove the rule. The now-celebrated 1901 July Fourth oration delivered in Chicago by the socialist Eugene

V. Debs was published in its entirety in the *Social Democratic Herald*. Debs, however, was a past and future candidate for the presidency, a national figure as much as Taft or Wilson though he did not hold office.[18]

Like Colt, the presidential orators systematically relegated the Revolution to the distant past. Roosevelt, speaking in Huntington, New York, in 1903, briefly invoked the "spirit of '76" and called on his listeners to live up to the example set by the heroes of the Revolutionary War. But he quickly turned from them to the more recent past of the Civil War, striking the supercessionist notes that had become common during the 1860s. The "veterans of 1861 and 1865 have a proprietary interest in this day that we now celebrate. For to them as much as to the men of '76 we owe the existence of this nation as a nation." The fusion of the Revolution and the Civil War was still a commonplace nearly forty years after the war for the Union had come to an end.[19] Wilson, who in 1918 used the occasion of the Fourth to give a speech about national self-determination, also relegated the Revolution to a relatively distant past. He compared the founders to the "barons at Runnymede," the medieval authors of Magna Carta. More pointedly, in an address that primarily focused on the need to spread national self-determination around the globe in the wake of the First World War, he declared that this question had been "settled for America" since the late eighteenth century. The sense of a stable and closed American revolutionary experience was unmistakable.[20]

Debs's 1901 speech, while its view of the United States was more critical than those of US presidents, presented a similar vision of the Revolution as a far-off relic. Debs began with a conventional evocation of the Declaration and its "proposition that men are created equal." He quickly widened the distance between the past and the present. "The Framers of the Constitution of this country had no faith in the people," he pronounced. He then outlined what he saw as the grave failings of the US political system and the tyranny of capital that had developed in the United States during the nineteenth century. He concluded by calling for another revolution—the revolution of socialism—which would ensure that "the wealth that is created is in the possession of the men who created it." Debs cheekily concluded by averring that "I like the 4th of July. It breathes a spirit of revolution." Yet this oft-quoted line did not mean that he saw socialism as a continuation of the American Revolution. Indeed, quite the reverse: He looked forward, toward another revolution, the "ultimate triumph of socialism," which he hoped would unweave much of the fabric of the American founding era.[21]

The notion of the Revolution as closed spurred orators to direct its message outward rather than inward. In what at first might seem like a throwback to the oratorical tradition of the first decades of the Republic's existence, orators during the 1890s and early twentieth century devoted a considerable portion of their addresses to commenting on foreign politics. A particular preoccupation of many orators was the internationalization of the Revolution and the political model it had created. In 1891, Josiah Quincy—a direct descendant of a leading figure in the Revolution—made this point in a Boston town oration titled "The Coming Peace." He began by observing, quite incorrectly, that "the Declaration of Independence was regarded in 1776 and long afterwards from a purely national point of view." Now it was essential to recognize its role in reshaping "relations between nations." At considerable length, he argued that the United States could provide a model for the end of warfare: The "federal system of government," he suggested, had "solved the political problem" of governing empires and diverse peoples. He envisioned a world in which a form of global federalism would reign universally, rendering war obsolete.[22]

Two years later, a member of the Philadelphia Bar, James Beck, offered a similar account of the Revolution as an exemplar for the world. For Beck, as for Quincy, American independence was no longer in question: "The United States has demonstrated its right to separate existence." Yet even though US independence was vindicated, the Declaration, whose central idea he summed up as the belief that "there was a rule of right and wrong . . . that regulated the intercourse of nations," still had relevance for the wider world. The vision of an international order based on rules and mutual respect, which he believed was embodied in the Declaration, was now "a new force in humanity." He hoped and expected that the operation of this principle would usher in a "period of perpetual peace" in the near future.[23]

As the themes of the orations shifted, the years around 1900 also saw a significant change in the place of orations within the larger Fourth of July ceremonies. Orations, which for much of the nineteenth century had frequently extended to forty-five minutes or an hour, were now more often closer to fifteen minutes. This was an example of a much broader shift in the culture of public speaking: The stemwinders of the nineteenth century gave way to much shorter public speeches as new media forms and amusements—especially spectatorial entertainments, from fairs to film and radio—became more popular. Yet as orations grew shorter, the rest of the festive apparatus on the Fourth, from singing and dancing to hearty drinking, continued unchanged. The effect was to gradually empty celebrations of the Fourth of what had been their main intellectual content.[24]

During the fifty years between the mid-1920s and the Bicentennial, presidential oratory thoroughly dominated the Fourth of July. Presidents had long participated in celebrations of the Fourth. But the centrality of their role in the twentieth century was a novelty. The Fourth in the long nineteenth century had been a local event shaped by individual communities—the leaders as well as the dissenters. When presidents took over Fourth of July oratory in the twentieth century, the holiday's rhetorical character became less rich; it was about the nation, full stop. This was a nation, moreover, whose stability and primacy the orators assumed. There was little sense of conflict or doubt in presidents' depictions of the nation on the Fourth.

Calvin Coolidge set the tone for this final transformation of Fourth of July oratory with his discourse on the one hundred and fiftieth anniversary, in 1926. The institutions of the Revolution, he began, had "met, and met successfully, the test of experiment." He narrated in detail the events and ideas that had led up to this "successful" Revolution, drawing heavily on the historically oriented oratorical strand that had achieved a kind of apotheosis in 1876. He ended his oration with a conclusion that envisioned the Revolution as fixed in amber. There is "a finality that is exceedingly restful" about the "Declaration," he declared. "No advance, no progress can be made beyond [its] propositions." This was the very inverse of the nineteenth-century vision of the constantly evolving Revolution, driven by the force of the Declaration. Coolidge's Declaration, by contrast, was hardly more than a beautiful mummy, a Revolution fixed in time and unchangeable.[25]

The 1926 anniversary marked a turning point as well in the practice of publishing orations in pamphlet form. Although a handful of orations continued to appear in print thereafter, at unpredictable intervals, these few pamphlets did not represent a continuation of the precentennial tradition. Even the orations delivered by presidents, which often had a national audience in mind, were only occasionally published in their entirety in newspapers and rarely in the form of separate pamphlets. Not even the one hundred and fiftieth anniversary in 1926 sparked any revival of the older publishing practice. Unlike in 1826, 1851, or 1876, there was no surge in the number of printed orations that year.[26]

A decade later, after the Depression and the New Deal had substantially repudiated the politics of the Coolidge era, the Fourth of July found Franklin D. Roosevelt espousing a vision of the Revolution just as sepia toned as his predecessor. Invited to Thomas Jefferson's Monticello in 1936, Roosevelt began his oration that year in a historical vein, recounting the lives of Jefferson and Benjamin Franklin. The president praised both for their "fertile minds" and their "genius." Their generation, in addition to having "established" the government under which America had "lived and grown" for a century and a half, had also been unique, "elevated above the common run of mankind." This led him to wonder, "Was . . . the spirit of a Golden Age gone now, and never to be repeated in our history?" Roosevelt answered with a qualified negative: "It is not beyond our power to re-light that sacred fire." Yet in spite of his seeming confidence that the flames of the revolutionary era could be rekindled, the sense of immense distance between the present and the past could hardly have been clearer.[27]

In the wake of World War II, presidents in the 1950s and 1960s turned back to the internationalist themes that had dominated Fourth of July oratory at the turn of the twentieth century. In his 1951 address from the grounds of the Washington Monument, Harry Truman drew extensive parallels between the Revolutionary War and the ongoing Korean War. The situation in 1951, he argued with rather pedantic detail, was "much like that of the Americans in 1776." Then they had been "launching a new kind of national government"; now the struggle was to create "a new kind of international organization."[28] Eleven years later, John F. Kennedy struck similar notes in his address at Independence Hall. Coming near the height of the Cold War, mere months before the Cuban Missile Crisis, Kennedy's speech revolved around the principles of national self-determination and independence. The president portrayed the United States as the eldest born of the independent nations, which now held the "leadership" of a "worldwide movement for independence." The Revolution of independence, complete in the United States for nearly two centuries, was now "coming to an end" in the rest of the world as well.[29]

The Bicentennial of the American Revolution in 1976, like the Centennial a century earlier, capped off and confirmed the transformations that had taken place in the rhetoric of the Fourth over the previous decades. Oratory was only a small part of the Bicentennial celebrations. The federal government had established a Bicentennial Commission in 1966 to begin planning events for the anniversary. The commission focused some of its attention on organizing large public events, along the lines of the Centennial Exposition. But it also devoted a great deal of effort to creating commercial and private-sector partnerships to publicize and monetize the Bicentennial. This commercial and often conservative-leaning plan for the Bicentennial elicited a considerable counterblast from the Left, with many organizations—official and semiofficial—offering counter-programming to the official Bicentennial. This included, among other things, public protests against pollution and civil rights demonstrations by Black, Native American, and gay and lesbian Americans.[30] Most of these events built primarily on the festive traditions of the Fourth rather than on its oratorical tradition.

For President Gerald Ford and his speechwriters, however, the Bicentennial did call for a number of Fourth of July speeches. They planned for him a series of short "remarks," in the now-familiar mode of presidential oratory, to be delivered around July Fourth at significant sites related to the Revolution, including the National Archives, Monticello, and Valley Forge.[31]

The discussions around the drafting of the speeches reveal how the president and his advisors framed the Revolution for themselves. The speechwriter David Gergen made a number of initial suggestions that harked back to the original nineteenth-century tradition. He suggested structuring the speeches around the venerable theme of the "American Experiment": an "experiment," he elaborated in terms that would have been familiar to an orator in 1815, "that each new generation must continue and pass on to its children." "Each of us," he concluded his recommendations, "is really a signer of the Declaration of Independence."[32] The conservative intellectual Irving Kristol, who was also consulted, urged the White House staff to examine speeches collected in a volume suggestively titled *America's Continuing Revolution*.[33]

It was telling, given these suggestions, that Robert Hartmann, the president's counselor responsible for speechwriting, overrode these proposals. He instead chose as the theme "The American Adventure." In a memo announcing the choice, he explained that "'adventure' conveys a sense of excitement and of continuation—the best is yet to be." As he informed the speechwriting staff, the goal was for each speech to "*look forward* more than backward in Bicentennial self-congratulation." The Revolution, in short, was almost to be ignored; what mattered was "the future."[34]

Whether in spite of these highly conventional features or because of them, Ford's Independence Day speeches were a failure—even from the point of view of their authors. In a memo dispatched on July 1, 1976, after Ford had delivered the first of his planned discourses, speechwriter David Gergen worried that the whole series of speeches would "[slip] under the wave without a sound." The "American Adventure," with its suggestion of an exciting future that was beginning, does not seem to have caught the public eye. Gergen's suggestion for how to fix the speeches only highlighted just how distant the Revolution now seemed: "We ought to consider," he wrote, "a speech that contains a coherent vision of the future."[35]

The Bicentennial and the failure of Ford's speeches signaled the final demise of the critical tradition of oratory on the Fourth of July that had been born in Boston two hundred years earlier, when American independence was just a year old.

For decades after the Bicentennial—even to this day—orators continued to step up to mark the Fourth in towns and cities around the country. Yet even where the practice of orations still exists, it is greatly diminished. Isolated speeches are, at best, threadbare shreds of the astonishingly dense and rich fabric of discourse that used to span the country. The orations that are delivered fall too often into the trap of self-confident self-congratulation. Or they take on a memorial cast, devoted to remembering the long-ago heroes and heroics of a bygone revolutionary age.

What has vanished from these orations is the central belief that animated speakers on the Fourth of July throughout the United States' first century. The idea, at once so strange and yet so simple, that both the orator and audience were participants in a living revolution: an ongoing political transformation in which they were actors, not spectators.

EPILOGUE

Fourth of July oratory may be mostly dead today, but its history still has much to offer us. Looking at how Americans reflected on revolution throughout the nation's first century revives long-standing questions about American nationhood and nationalism—and about the contested character of the Revolution itself and the Republic it created.

To Americans in the nineteenth century, the Revolution and the Republic were fragile creations. Historians have long looked at American nationalism, the idea and the discourse of national feeling, in much the same way that they have studied European nationalism of the same era. On both sides of the Atlantic, scholars have tended to find an increasingly elaborate construction of the nation that elicited fierce attachment and immense national pride. There is no question that this is accurate, as far as it goes. Americans in the nineteenth century were certainly nationalistic: proud of their country, assertive about its uniqueness and importance, and increasingly ready to see themselves as on a mission to dominate the hemisphere. In this sense, American nationalism was not all that different from European imperialism of the same era, with its self-appointed "civilizing" missions and brutal projects of colonial domination.

But American nationalism, at least, had another side that has been largely forgotten, which rings out with great clarity in the orations delivered on the Fourth of July. This reverse side of nationalism saw the American "experiment" as something at once profoundly valuable and thoroughly vulnerable. There were a number of elements that generated this sense of fragility: the human and geographic diversity of the nation, its relative youth, and the powerful stresses of foreign powers and internal divisions. It found voice in orators' constant worries about the durability of the United States and its republican institutions, and in the annual hand-wringing about the dangers—first external, then internal—that threatened to unravel the nation. The fact that many of these fears were realized in the 1860s with the outbreak of the Civil War underscores that they were not idle or baseless worries. Even if the orators' rhetoric sometimes seemed overblown, they were in the end not far off the mark.

The feeling of fragility that haunted American nationalism may help to explain some of the particularities of the US role on the global stage during the nineteenth and early twentieth centuries. Though Americans were in many respects highly emulative of Europeans, their embrace of colonial empire was for a long time very tentative. Colonialism, as it was practiced by Europeans in this period, entailed the creation of layers of colonial authority that subordinated the colonies to the metropole, an approach that generated its own kinds of fragility and division. Americans avoided this. American expansion in the West and abroad, until the very last years of the nineteenth century, was predicated on fully integrating new territories into the nation. Americans were eager to commercially dominate neighboring regions—including much of the Caribbean and South America. But if these regions were not going to become part of the United States, Americans did not wish to exercise any direct political control over them. The current of fear that ran icy cold through Americans' sense of their national identity made it hard to imagine any further extension of the already stretched-out national structure.[1]

In the nineteenth century, Americans' view of themselves as a cohesive people also began to change. An old view, which dates back to the Federalists in opposition during the early nineteenth century holds that the story of American peoplehood was a process of consolidation. Out of groups of colonial subjects in the late eighteenth century who shared little beyond their dislike of an overbearing British government, a common culture and a set of shared institutions gradually developed. This idea of a homogeneous American nation, underpinned by a shared culture steeped in Protestantism, has had a remarkable revival in the early twenty-first century. An opposing view is that early America was characterized by diversity, with different groups—Black, white, and Native; immigrant and native-born—developing their own versions of an American culture. These peoples coexisted, often uneasily or in conflict, but alongside one another. Yet both of these visions rest on a strong belief that Americans are those born on American soil or who have come to it—a flexible but still constraining form of blood-and-soil nationhood.

As nineteenth-century American orators thought aloud about the Revolution and the nation that had sprung from it, however, they suggested another, much more capacious version of American peoplehood. References to birthplace and lineage, though they did appear in orations from time to time, were only sometimes employed in an exclusionary sense. The American peoplehood that the orators imagined could extend well beyond the boundaries of North America, embracing seemingly any person who shared a commitment to the principles of the Revolution. And it was a peoplehood that was multigenerational as well, continually renewed as successive generations in turn lay their own claims to American nationality. In this sense, it was as immediate in time as it was fluid in space—a peoplehood that was readily extensible because it was grounded in the present and in principles, not in the distant past.[2]

And what of the sense many Americans had that they were participants in an ongoing revolution? It has long been an article of faith for many that Americans are peculiarly immune to revolutionary enthusiasm. Unlike the French, they argue, Americans were neither inclined nor impelled toward dramatic upheavals and overthrows of the existing political system. Yet for decades, year in and year out during the nineteenth century, Americans on the Fourth of July refuted this fantasy of US political conservatism. On the Fourth, the Revolution became a living presence. Orators encouraged their audiences to see themselves as actors in a revolutionary movement that was still ongoing, in which the possibilities for dramatic change remained open. Indeed, for many Americans—particularly the abolitionists fighting against the institution of slavery—the idea that the Revolution was still in progress was an essential part of their moral vision. Only by continuing the revolutionary struggle, through the abolition of slavery, could the nation be saved from its terrible failure to live up to its own ideals.[3]

The belief that they were revolutionaries engaged in a struggle for radical transformation gave nineteenth-century American political movements a formidable energy. From abolitionists to temperance activists, advocates of workingmen's rights to tribunes of religious liberty—all these movements lay claim to the mantle of the American Revolution, not merely as its heirs but as its actors. Few of them were interested in offering the kind of systematic—and often dogmatic—doctrines of permanent revolution that characterized European revolutionary movements of the nineteenth and early twentieth centuries. But that did not make them any less fierce in their embrace of the revolutionary struggle.

The long comet tail of the American Revolution released a final, terrible burst of energy during the Civil War and Reconstruction. This did not exactly mark the reopening of a "Founding era" that had already been closed and completed. For many of the war's protagonists, the Revolution had never really ended. The Civil War and Reconstruction were the culmination of a transformation that had begun in the late eighteenth century. They fulfilled the promises made in the Declaration of Independence and marked the completion of the long struggle to secure the independence and durability of the United States in the face of external threats and internal dangers. The apotheosis of the American Revolution during Reconstruction was far from perfect, to be sure. Yet as orators signaled with their swift and decisive turn toward memorialization, in 1876 and after, something that had long been underway had now come to an end.

Is the American Revolution still underway in 2026? Will it be so in 2076 or 3026? These questions may seem absurd. Of course the American Revolution is over. If it did not end in 1783, then it certainly ended with the writing of the Constitution. If not then, then with the War of 1812. Or at the latest, if one really wished to stretch it, with the Civil War. Even to speak of the American Revolution as an ongoing concern in the twenty-first century can seem unreal.

Yet in light of the history we have traced in the previous pages, to ask whether the Revolution is still at work—and what its future might be—is not only plausible but also necessary. Throughout the nineteenth century, for many decades after the treaty of peace that established the independence of the United States, a striking number of Americans believed that the Revolution was still in progress. The Republic it had created, many of them said, remained an "experiment." It had a perpetually uncertain future, which was at once a wellspring of immense hopes for the future and a source of profound anxiety.

The American Revolution was not just a string of events that had taken place in the distant past—at least not in the way that Fourth of July orators spoke of it. It was as much an idea as an event. A set of beliefs and commitments, of ways of looking at the world and envisioning what it can become. The Revolution, seen from this angle, has no natural ending point. It has no necessary or natural chronology that constrains it to the eighteenth or nineteenth centuries.

Asking whether the Revolution is over is, therefore, really a way of asking whether we believe that the Revolution's goals have been accomplished. Have its ideas and ideals achieved their fullest possible development? In this sense, surely, the Revolution is still in progress in our day. And it does not and will not end of its own accord. The Revolution ends only when we decide, collectively, that its aspirations—and ours—are fulfilled.

A VISUAL ANALYSIS OF FOURTH OF JULY ORATIONS, 1777–1876

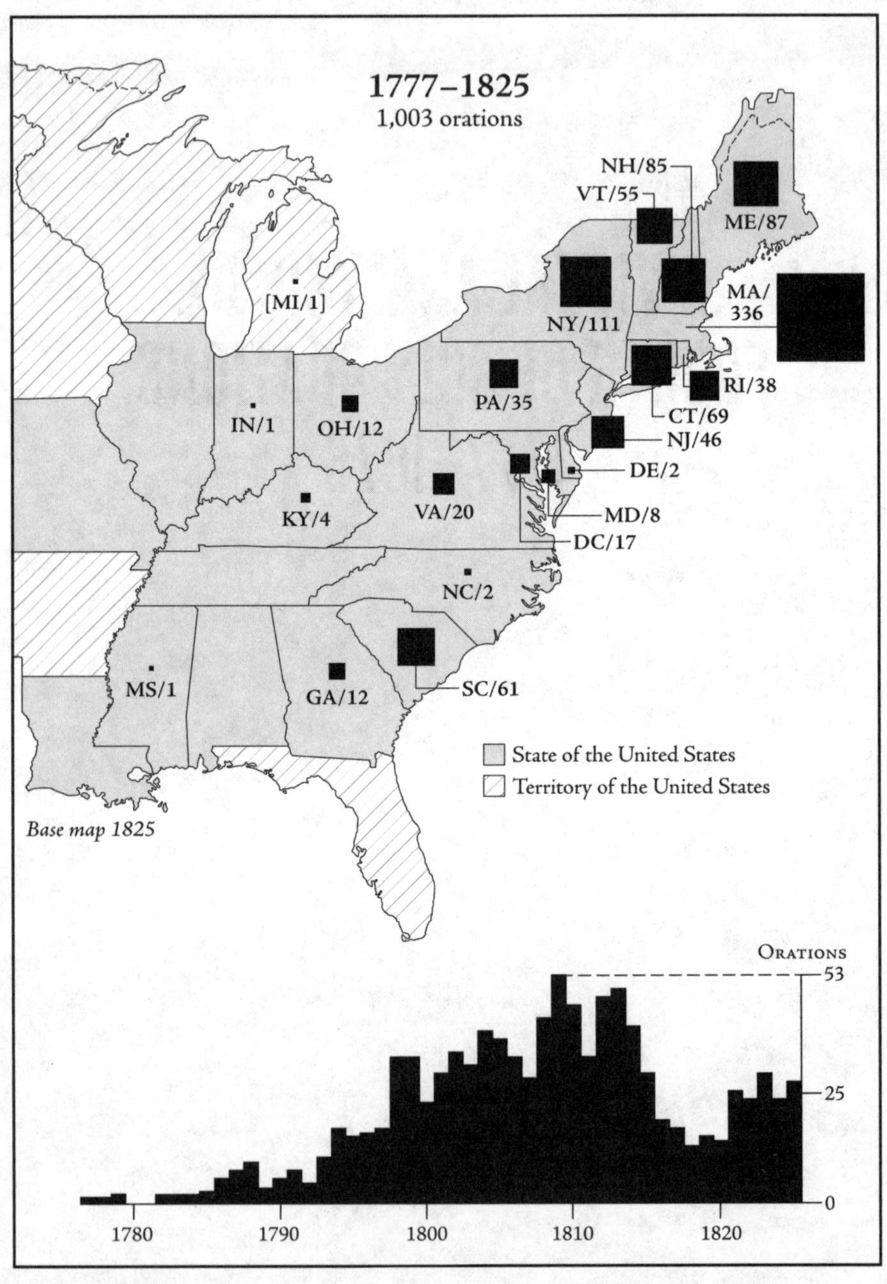

Fourth of July orations delivered in North America and published as pamphlets, 1777–1825, by state and by year.

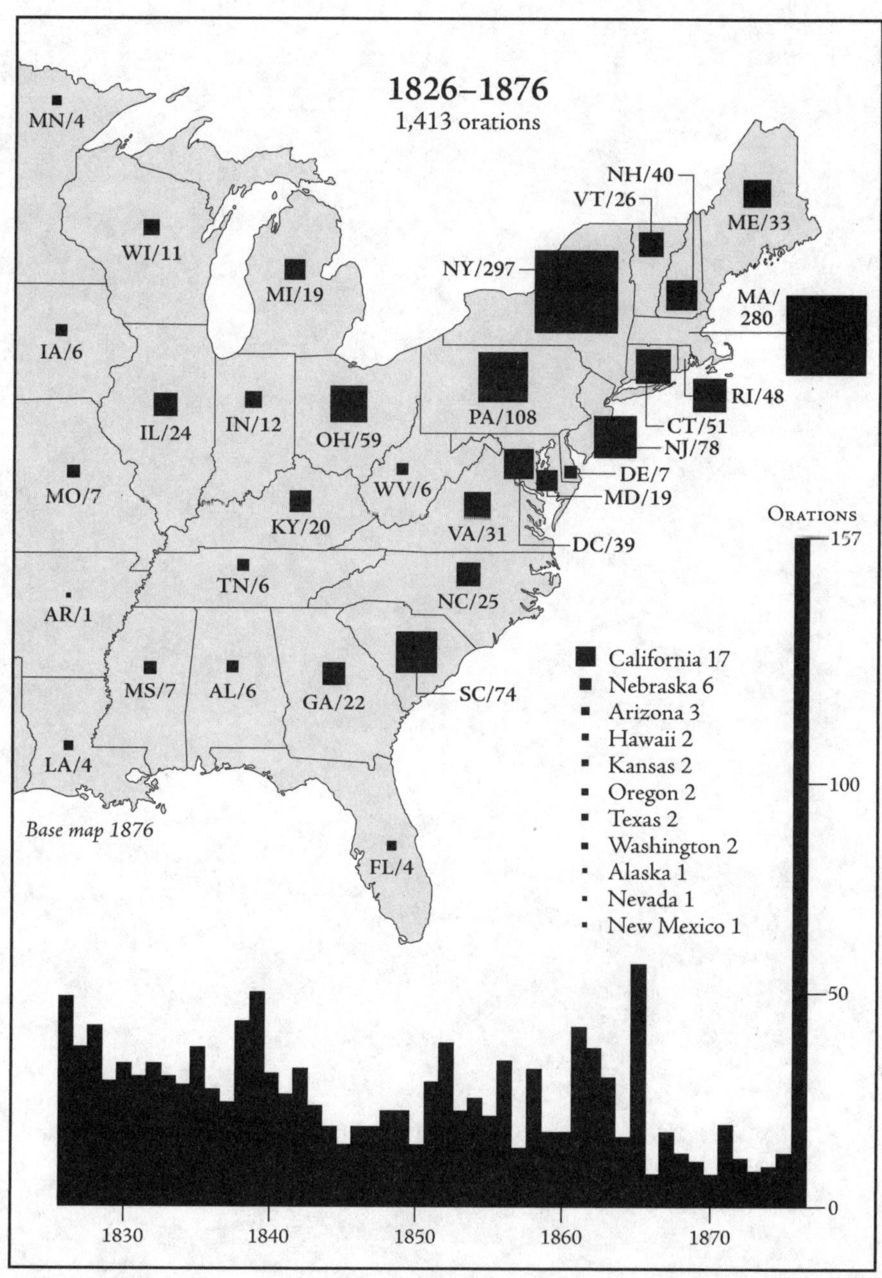

Fourth of July orations delivered in North America and published as pamphlets, 1825–1876, by state and by year.

APPENDIX

A SELECTION OF ORATIONS

ZECHARIAH LEWIS

*An Oration on the Apparent, and the Real Political Situation in the United States (New Haven, Connecticut, 1799)**

The author of this oration, of strong Federalist sympathies, graduated from Yale College in 1794. He was licensed to preach in 1796 but became an editor in 1799, ultimately based in New York.[1] *The conclusion of his oration, reproduced here, expresses the fear that foreign invasion or influence would destroy the Republic. As was typical, Lewis grounded these worries in comparisons with foreign places, particularly Europe.*

THUS, my Fellow-Citizens, foreign attachments, and foreign influence; the introduction and spread of demoralizing principles; and the prejudices and passions of many of our own people, are the principal sources of the dangers, with which our Country is so imminently threatened. Against these we should ever guard with united vigilance, activity, and firmness.

---

* Zechariah Lewis, *An Oration on the Apparent, and the Real Political Situation in the United States* (Thomas Green & Son, 1799).

CAST your eyes again on Europe. Behold her Republics, through these sources, seduced, oppressed, and destroyed. Forget not that even happy protestant Switzerland, "where religion and freedom had reared their sacred head in the palace and in the hamlet," was deluged by the same storm, which is now gathering over your own Country, and portending its destruction. In the character of independent nations, the European Republics no longer exist. The same arts, intrigues and deceptions, which hastened their ruin, you have to oppose. Their enemies have become yours. In their mournful history, you may read your own danger, your interest, and your duty.

YOU will be told "that you are not in danger—that the alarm is false—a disingenuous fabrication—the mere effusion of party zeal." Alas! how often was this baneful lesson taught, as well by honest, as by artful and designing men, to the deluded inhabitants of Geneva and Switzerland! How were they thus led on, from one degradation to another, until the eventful blow was struck, which stript them of their national character, their religion, and freedom—which exposed to the most brutal violence their wives and their daughters—and drenched their streets with the blood of their Fathers, their Brothers, and their Sons! Americans! if you do not learn wisdom from their example, your ruin is inevitable. Slumber not in fatal security, while your enemies are within your gates, corrupting and poisoning the very sources of your happiness. Remember that the unprincipled monster, which has already devoured every Republic on earth, your own only excepted, although he stalks over the world with rapid and detested strides, never shows his brazen front, until groveling through secret and filthy avenues, he has corrupted the manners, morals, and religion; soothed, flattered, and blinded the people; divided and enervated their government, and thus BROKEN DOWN THEIR WALLS AND THEIR BULWARKS.

TRISTRAM BURGES

Liberty, Glory and Union, or American Independence
*(Providence, Rhode Island, 1810)**

The author, a figure in the Federalist party in Rhode Island, served in a variety of political offices over a quarter century, including as a Representative in Congress. His oration is highly critical of the Jefferson administration and paints a dark picture of the nation. To maintain US independence and sovereignty, he says, his listeners must embrace three "great principles of the revolution" and make them "the principles of our government."

OUR Independence has given a new era to the world. The first day which shone upon it is now celebrated by Americans, and the friends of Americans, in every quarter of the globe. We solemnize this day; it is our country's festival; and shall be immortal as our national sovereignty. The revolution, originating our political existence, was one of those mighty events which break on the world, to the delight and astonishment of mankind. As if the nations of the earth

* Tristram Burges, *Liberty, Glory and Union, or American Independence* (Dunham & Hawkins, 1810).

had stood around the shores of the Atlantick, and beheld, bursting from the misty bosom of its heaving waves, a broad region, towering with mountains, waving with forests, green with wide plains, glittering with spiry cities, and swarming with numerous and busy population. Thus they beheld the American revolution.

. . .

. . . [L]iberty, glory, and union were the three great principles of the revolution; and national freedom, national honour, and national unanimity were consummated in the Independence of our country. What think you, my fellow-citizens, could we have effected without these illustrious passions? What would have been our councils; where the fields of our fame; what the result of our toils and wars? Aided by them the world was soon filled with our renown; the wisdom of our statesmen, the exploits of our heroes; the war was terminated; America triumphed; and sat down among the nations of the earth, to enjoy Independence and peace.

Do you ask how shall that Independence be preserved, and rendered perpetual? By the preservation of those things, without which, it could not have been acquired. Was a love of liberty necessary? Then let us love liberty. Was a love of national glory? Then let us love the honour, the glory of our country. Was a spirit of union? Then let us be united. The principles of our revolution should be the principles of our government; and, so long as they are, we shall be independent; but, when they are abandoned, we must abandon our sovereignty.

. . .

Indeed we are fallen into a forlorn condition. We have widely departed from the principles of the revolution; and union, and glory, and liberty are departing from us. Our constitution has been violated; profligate foreigners receive the prerogatives of citizens; our union is enfeebled by extending our territory; the national navy is hewn down to gun-boats, American seamen reduced to galley slavery; an embargo has licked up the very dust of the treasury; the country is impoverished, exhausted, and depressed; while French partialities, French principles, and French influence, have brought our nation, almost to the foot of that proud tyrant, who now rides on the shoulders of Europe. Is there no refuge, no defence? Yes, my countrymen.

Let us look back to what achieved our Independence. Those immortal principles will ever preserve it.

HENRY WHEATON, ESQ.

An Oration delivered before the Tammany Society . . .
*(Providence, Rhode Island, 1810)**

When he delivered this oration, the author was a young lawyer, an ally of the then-dominant Republican Party, at the start of what would become a prominent career including stints as publisher of the US Supreme Court's decisions and as a US diplomat. His speech, like that of his Federalist counterpart Burges, which was delivered on the same day in the same city, stresses the need to maintain US sovereignty and independence in the face of foreign influence and attacks.

. . . And shall we, my countrymen, in the maturity of our national strength; with the rich resources accumulated in a long period of peace and prosperity; and when we have acquired a name and a rank among the nations,—shall we bow our necks to that yoke which our ancestors disdained; and to avoid submission to which, they endured so many privations, made so many sacrifices, resisted so many temptations, and overcome such formidable obstacles? Has the

* Henry Wheaton, Esq., *An Oration delivered before the Tammany Society . . .* (Phenix Press, 1810).

soul-subduing spirit of avarice so benumbed us, that we are insensible of shame; lost to glory; and forgetful of the deeds of our ancestors? Their history reads to us a lesson, which, if we have understandings to comprehend, or hearts to feel, cannot be wholly lost upon us. It admonishes us to union; it speaks in a voice of indignation to our contending factions, and commands them to be still; to cease their rude clamors, and to sacrifice upon the altar of their country their mischievous passions. It invokes the genius of patriotism to shine forth, and dissipate the mists of prejudice, and the noxious vapors of foreign influence, which infect our air with contagion; eradicate from our hearts the last lingering sentiment of love to our native land; and stifle in our bosoms every feeling of national pride. Notwithstanding the horrors and sufferings of our revolution; notwithstanding the multiplied wrongs we have ever since endured from Britain, and which make the cheek to burn with shame at a recital of them; yet a British influence has silently and imperceptibly gained a control in our country. It has perplexed and dashed our maturest counsels; has again and again threatened to break in pieces our national union, and to involve us in a British alliance; that grave which yawns to swallow up our independence. It has excited a false and delusive cry of a French influence, to divert the attention of the people from its own dangerous arts. It has dared to accuse the author of the Declaration of Independence; the man who had been the foremost to incur the certain vengeance of our enemies had they succeeded in reducing us to slavery; of being a traitor to his country, and sold to a foreign power.

. . .

Let not freedom faint and expire in this her last asylum. To us is committed the charge of sustaining her sacred flame. If it is here extinguished, "we know not where is that Promethean heat that can its light relume." Ages of slavery and darkness may intervene, before the world is again revived and cheered with its beneficent rays. . . . Independence is not to be taken up as an idle pageant, and laid down again with childish inconstancy. Nor can it be yielded in fragments, first to one power, and then to another. By blood and toil obtained, by vigilance and fortitude must it be defended and preserved. It is the prize of successful valor; and rapacity is ever ready to wrest it from the unsteady grasp of weakness. The great object for which nations have ever been contending, and for which we see a world in arms, is the power to manage their own affairs without foreign interference or controul [*sic*]. And if there be an object worth contention, it is surely this. It is the sense of national independence, in which the energy and free spirit of a people, and all that is great and patriotic, reside; and without which, a nation becomes poor, and languid, sunk and degraded, even in its own esteem.

ORVILLE LUTHER HOLLEY

*An Oration (Lyons, New York, 1822)**

The author, a newspaper editor, is most famous for having printed the original text of "The Night Before Christmas," which appeared in his paper, the Troy Sentinel, *in 1823. In this oration, Holley takes the typical tour of other countries, including (just before this passage), France, Spain, Russia, and Greece. He then offers a long and remarkably positive view of independent Haiti, which, though marred by references to Black inferiority, concludes with a remarkable vision of a free, Black-dominated, republican Caribbean. Throughout, in his comparisons with Haiti, he hints at the dangers and immorality of slavery in the United States.*

On our own continent, also, tyranny has again suffered discomfiture, and liberty has given charters to three new nations. More than half Christendom—notwithstanding the boasted superiority and energy of monarchical institutions, and in the face of confederate kings—more than half Christendom has been already placed under the dominion of republican institutions.

---

* Orville Luther Holley, *An Oration, On the Permanency of Republican Institutions* (H. T. Day, 1822).

In this connection, moreover, I cannot omit to mention the independent republic of Hayti. In the island of St. Domingo, my fellow citizens, a political phenomenon has been exhibited, unexampled in the annals of human society. The descendants and survivors of those unhappy creatures, who were compelled by fraud and violence, to pass from the liberty of innocent, though unenlightened and barren barbarism, through the horrors of the Middle Passage, to galling and uncompensated bondage, have been enabled by God's good providence to throw off their fetters, and rise from the ignominy of their thraldom, to the dignity and hopes of personal freedom and political independence. When the history of the negro race in America, is liberally viewed, it assumes an interest of a most singular and romantic character. The establishment of an independent government within the pale of Christendom, and in the centre of the commercial world, by slaves from Africa, is surely to be ranked among the remarkable events of this wonderful era; and though accomplished by violence, and attended by circumstances of desperate guilt, it is nevertheless an event which retributive justice cannot but sanction, and which the sincere philanthropist may justly hail, as another and a mighty stride in the general melioration of mankind. For the negroes, it is the first invincible proof, palpable to all, which they have been enabled to exhibit to a contemptuous or pitying world, that their Creator had a good destiny in store for them . . .

If considered without prejudice, no revolution furnishes so much matter to arrest attention, and compel men to pause and ponder, as that of St. Domingo; and by none has the vigor of human nature—paradoxical as it may sound—been so strikingly exemplified. Ignorant, and consequently degraded, as the majority of slaves in that island were; without any aid from experience, and destitute of the multiplied resources of a cultivated state of society; but writhing under cruelty, and dimly discerning the reason why they might lawfully rise against oppression; by the mere force of simple but energetic human nature, they threw off the incumbent load of servitude; they started from bondage, and standing elate upon the high places of freedom, they shook their broken chains, astonished at themselves, and filling the world with wonder. Notwithstanding the disadvantages of their condition, and the obstacles thrown in their way by the jealousy and pride of other nations, they have confirmed their sovereignty. They have cultivated successfully the arts of peace, as well as of war; commerce has prospered with them; and they have already done much toward providing for their own education and moral advancement. . . .

The institutions which these black men have at last established, are republican; and the period is not far distant when all the European dependencies in this hemisphere, must become sovereign states; black or white, they will at last assume independence, and they will be independent republics. Of these dependencies in the West-Indies, by far the greatest portion of the population being black, though the government and property of the islands are at present in the hands of white men, yet, when the separation of the colonies from the mother countries shall take place, and their governments shall be revolutionized, the wealth and power will be transferred to the negroes. Not only does the example of St. Domingo indicate such a result, but it is prognosticated by the whole history of colonization. The color of the skin affects not the elements of human nature, nor the principles upon which men rise from subjection to sovereignty, and move on from ignorance to knowledge and refinement.

ELIAKIM PHELPS

*An address, delivered before the Geneva Abstinence Society, on Sabbath evening, July 4, 1830 (Geneva, New York, 1830)**

A typical anti-alcohol (temperance) oration, which draws elaborate and mostly unconvincing parallels between the Revolution and the struggle against drinking. This oration exemplifies some of the tendencies of the more individualistic form of the "inward turn" of the 1820s and 1830s—namely, a focus on personal moral reform as a path to national salvation and a thoroughly religious vocabulary.

[A]n enemy more formidable, a hundred fold, than all the power of Britain united, is at this moment carrying on a most disastrous warfare against the liberties of our country. . . . *This enemy is Intemperance.*

As this day stands intimately connected, by all its associations, with the incidents of the revolution, I shall attempt a comparison between the evils of which our country had *then*

---

* Eliakim Phelps, *An address, delivered before the Geneva Abstinence Society, on Sabbath evening, July 4, 1830* (James Bogert, 1830).

to complain from British aggression, and those of which she has *now* to complain from the ravages of Intemperance.

. . .

To redeem our country from the evil of Intemperance, calls as loudly for united and persevering effort, as did the emergencies of the country in '76. On this point, my argument is simply this: We have, according to the most accurate computation, at this time three hundred thousand drunkards in our land; and such is the emergency of our country at this very time, that without united and persevering effort to arrest the evil, we are an undone people. The question then before us, is one of *life* and *death*: it is, whether we shall, as a nation, *live* or *die*: it is, whether we shall continue, as an independent nation, to maintain that proud and dignified attitude which we already have acquired; or whether we shall add to all our other sins, the guilt of national suicide, and, like Samson, grasp the pillars which sustain the fair fabric of our independence, and, with our own hands, bury ourselves and our children in the mighty ruins. . . . Every lover of his country, and every friend of her institutions, is bound, in duty as a patriot, to exert his influence to the utmost, to arrest the progress of this evil. This is not the work of ministers alone, nor of churches alone, nor of societies alone: it is the work of the whole nation. The salvation of our country is staked upon the issue. We make the appeal, then, to all. We appeal to you as patriots, and in the name of our common country. As you value her blood-bought liberties, and as you prize her invaluable institutions, we entreat you to come up to the help.

. . .

Let [the Fourth], then, from this time forward, be sacredly consecrated to our country's renovation. And, when in after times, your children and your children's children shall assemble on this anniversary, to recount the deeds of the revolutionary worthies, let them be able to say, On this day, also, did our fathers, of a later generation, declare and maintain a SECOND INDEPENDENCE, which delivered our fair heritage, forever, from the horrors, and miseries, and calamities of Intemperance!

FRANCES WRIGHT

An Address to the People of Philadelphia
*(Philadelphia, Pennsylvania, 1829)**

The author, a Scottish-born social and political reformer who became enamored of the United States during her twenties, was one of the few women who delivered Fourth of July orations in the first half of the nineteenth century. This speech offers a searing rebuke of Americans, calling their revolution "incomplete and insufficient" and summoning them to recommit to the "principles" of the Declaration.

High is the ground you have assumed, people of the United States! Pure and sublime are the principles on which you have based your institutions. Simple and grand are those institutions themselves. And, in proportion to the greatness of these, is your responsibility.

Other nations, governed by the loose tide of circumstances, or by the whim of silly monarchs and their crafty ministers, may throw from them the folly of their national errors, or claim but little part in their wiser actions. Not

* Frances Wright, *An Address to the People of Philadelphia* (G. Evans, 1829).

so with you, people of these United States! You have willed yourselves free as well as independent. You are proclaimed to the world for a self governing people. You have declared liberty to be the birthright of man. You have purchased it with toil, and blood, and suffering; entrenched it within the peaceful but immutable bulwarks of representative government, and hold in your hands the power to correct its every error, and to improve its every good.

Behold, then, every institution, every law, every action of your government emanating from yourselves! Is the spirit of the national policy enlightened—on you reflects the honor. Are the public measures wise—to you is traced the wisdom. Is aught done foolishly—the folly rests with your ignorance. Is aught neglected—with your negligence lies the omission. You may not, then, be judged in comparison with other nations. Your own mouth must supply your sentence. Even by those principles shall you be tried, which are set forth in this declaration; and to the support of which, you, even as your fathers before you, have pledged your lives, your fortunes, and your honor.

If, then, in your constitutional code, there should be found one article in violation of the principles herein enshrined, then is your sacred honor impeached in the eyes of the world. If, in one act of your government, at home or abroad, you shall have violated these principles, then is your sacred honor impeached in the eyes of the world. If you shall have harbored within your bosom, and sanctioned by your laws, one practice outraging these principles, then is your sacred honor impeached in the eyes of the world. If ye shall have omitted one measure necessary for the poctection [*sic*] and practical illustration of these principles, then is your sacred honor impeached in the eyes of the world.

How stands, then, your account, my fellow citizens? How have ye fulfilled your promise and redeemed your pledge? Can ye, on this day, when the eyes of the world are upon ye, renew your solemn appeal to all the nations of the earth, and court their scrutiny throughout your borders? Can ye, on this day, challenge the investigation of mankind, and say—"We have improved the heritage bequeathed by our father. We have followed the path they traced for our footsteps. We have revealed, in our practice, the excellence of those truths whose theory they proclaimed. We have exercised those rights and powers which they purchased with their blood, and gave us, in peace to enjoy, and in wisdom to improve?"

Can ye, fellow citizens, say this? Oh—would, for the sake of humankind, that ye could answer "Yea!"

Bitter are the words of reproof; nor needs it that my voice should speak them. The cry of misery hath gone up from the land; and that cry is your condemnation.

And was it for this your fathers raised the standard of rebellion? Was it for this they braved an empire's power, and bare with ten years of war and tribulation? Was it to effect no more of good than we see around us, that they shut their unarmed ports against the navies of Britain, and set at nought the authorities of ancient days and the threats of parliaments and thrones? Was it to exchange the open tyranny of temporal kings for the more subtle dominion of spiritual hierarchs, that the American people first pledged their honor to this sacred instrument? Was it to build up the ascendancy of priests omniscient by the grace of God, that they challenged the prerogatives of monarchs omnipotent by the same? Was it to crush down the sons and daughters of your country's industry under the accumulated and accumulating evils of neglect, poverty, vice, starvation, and disease, that your fathers bought your independence with their blood, and decreed, by this charter, your equality as citizens, and your liberty as men? Oh! were this noble instrument to work no more of practical reform than it hath wrought to this hour, wiser it were to burn it on the very spot where sages first conceived and heroes proclaimed it, than longer to mock the ears of this nation and the hopes of the world with the sound of truths man is never to realize . . .

. . .

Until this great oversight be rectified [lack of education], the revolution we this day commemorate will be incomplete and insufficient; the "declaration" contained in this instrument will be void.

FREDERICK DOUGLASS

*Oration delivered in Corinthian Hall, Rochester, by Frederick Douglass, July 5th, 1852 (Rochester, New York, 1852)**

Born into slavery in Maryland around 1817, Frederick Douglass educated himself and escaped from bondage during the 1830s. By the time he gave this oration to an antislavery meeting in upstate New York, he was already a prominent member of the US abolitionist movement. His oration, while an exceptional piece of rhetoric, displays many of the hallmarks of earlier orations, including the critical tone, focus on the present day, and use of foreign comparisons.

My business, if I have any here to-day, is with the present. The accepted time with God and his cause is the ever-living now.

. . .

Fellow-citizens, pardon me, allow me to ask, why am I called upon to speak here to-day? What have I, or those I represent, to do with your national independence? Are the great principles of political freedom and of natural justice,

---

* Frederick Douglass, *Oration delivered in Corinthian Hall, Rochester, by Frederick Douglass, July 5th, 1852. Published by Request* (Lee, Mann & Co., 1852).

embodied in that Declaration of Independence, extended to us? and am I, therefore, called upon to bring our humble offering to the national altar, and to confess the benefits and express devout gratitude for the blessings resulting from your independence to us?

Would to God, both for your sakes and ours, that an affirmative answer could be truthfully returned to these questions! . . .

But, such is not the state of the case. I say it with a sad sense of the disparity between us. I am not included within the pale of this glorious anniversary! Your high independence only reveals the immeasurable distance between us. The blessings in which you, this day, rejoice, are not enjoyed in common.—The rich inheritance of justice, liberty, prosperity and independence, bequeathed by your fathers, is shared by you, not by me. The sunlight that brought life and healing to you, has brought stripes and death to me. This Fourth July is yours, not mine. You may rejoice, I must mourn. To drag a man in fetters into the grand illuminated temple of liberty, and call upon him to join you in joyous anthems, were inhuman mockery and sacrilegious irony. Do you mean, citizens, to mock me, by asking me to speak to-day? If so, there is a parallel to your conduct. And let me warn you that it is dangerous to copy the example of a nation whose crimes, towering up to heaven, were thrown down by the breath of the Almighty, burying that nation in irrecoverable ruin! I can to-day take up the plaintive lament of a peeled and woe-smitten people!

. . .

Fellow citizens; above your national, tumultuous joy, I hear the mournful wail of millions! whose chains, heavy and grievous yesterday, are, to-day, rendered more intolerable by the jubilee shouts that reach them. . . . I shall see, this day, and its popular characteristics, from the slave's point of view. Standing, there, identified with the American bondman, making his wrongs mine, I do not hesitate to declare, with all my soul, that the character and conduct of this nation never looked blacker to me than on this 4th of July! Whether we turn to the declarations of the past, or to the professions of the present, the conduct of the nation seems equally hideous and revolting. America is false to the past, false to the present, and solemnly binds herself to be false to the future. Standing with God and the crushed and bleeding slave on this occasion, I will, in the name of humanity which is outraged, in the name of liberty which is fettered, in the name of the constitution and the Bible, which are disregarded and trampled upon, dare to call in question and to denounce, with all the emphasis I can command, everything that serves to perpetuate slavery—the great sin and shame of America! "I will not equivocate; I will not excuse;" I will use the severest language I can command; and yet not one word shall escape me that any man, whose judgment is not blinded by prejudice, or who is not at heart a slaveholder, shall not confess to be right and just.

. . .

What, to the American slave, is your 4th of July? I answer; a day that reveals to him, more than all other days in the year, the gross injustice and cruelty to which he is the constant victim. To him, your celebration is a sham; your boasted liberty, an unholy license; your national greatness, swelling vanity; your sounds of rejoicing are empty and heartless; your denunciations of tyrants, brass fronted impudence; your shouts of liberty and equality, hollow mockery; your prayers and hymns, your sermons and thanksgivings, with all your religious parade, and solemnity, are, to him, mere bombast, fraud, deception, impiety, and hypocrisy—a thin veil to cover up crimes which would disgrace a nation of savages. There is not a nation on the earth guilty of practices, more shocking and bloody, than are the people of these United States, at this very hour.

Go where you may, search where you will, roam through all the monarchies and despotisms of the old world, travel through South America, search out every abuse, and when you have found the last, lay your facts by the side of the every day practices of this nation, and you will say with me, that, for revolting barbarity and shameless hypocrisy, America reigns without a rival.

. . .

I, therefore, leave off where I began, with hope. While drawing encouragement from "the Declaration of Independence," the great principles it contains, and the genius of American Institutions, my spirit is also cheered by the obvious tendencies of the age. Nations do not now stand in the same relation to each other that they did ages ago. No nation can now shut itself up, from the surrounding world, and trot round in the same old path of its fathers without interference. The time was when such could be done. Long established customs of hurtful character could formerly fence themselves in, and do their evil work with social impunity. Knowledge was then confined and enjoyed by the privileged few, and the multitude walked on in mental darkness. But a change has now come over the affairs of mankind. Walled cities and empires have become unfashionable. The arm of commerce has borne away the gates of the strong city. Intelligence is penetrating the darkest corners of the globe. It makes its pathway over and under the sea, as well as on the earth. Wind, steam, and lightning are its chartered agents. Oceans no longer divide, but link nations together. From Boston to London is now a holiday excursion. Space is comparatively annihilated.—Thoughts expressed on one side of the Atlantic, are distinctly heard on the other.

WALTER CLARKE

*"The state of the country." An oration delivered at Buffalo, July 4th, 1862 (Buffalo, New York, 1862)**

Referring to the "second nativity" of American liberty in the Civil War, the orator argues that the "founders of the Republic" had won liberty for the nation, but that this had to be complemented with "loyalty" in order to endure. Acquiring loyalty would "complet[e] the fabric which the fathers commenced"—bringing the revolutionary process to a close at long last.

But the Republic, which came into existence, in that first act of independence, has reached at length the period of its second nativity: and existing events fraught with all imaginable destinies for the future, summon us from the cradle, where Liberty was born, to the scene of present agony, where the same Liberty is passing through the anguish and the fear of a second birth.

. . .

---

* Walter Clarke, *"The state of the country." An oration delivered at Buffalo, July 4th, 1862* (Breed, Butler & Co., 1862).

But the founders of the Republic understood as we do, that it was essential to the stability of a free government, nay to its very existence indeed, that liberty should be balanced and harmonized by another sentiment of equal strength and equal purity, the sentiment, to wit, of Loyalty.

. . .

Our fathers gave us liberty. They could not give us loyalty also. For, while freedom is a social condition, into which we can be put by others—allegiance on the other hand is a popular sentiment, which we must unfold for ourselves, and a public habit which we must exercise in person. The fathers did what they could; gave us liberty, and defining in the charter which conveyed the costly inheritance, the loyalty which we must acquire and practice, left us to gain that wanting sentiment, by whatever discipline the future should chance to furnish. . . . Till the people could attain to a loyalty which should equal their rights, and be as cheerfully obedient, as they were willingly free, our fathers relied upon the force of the oath to make them submissive, and orderly, and true.

Independence had been achieved, liberty acquired, and the Nation conducted safely through the first stadium of its history, it must now enter upon a new probation and pass the ordeal of a second stage. The fathers had undertaken with their virtues, to acquire liberty for themselves and their children. Now the nation starting upon a new career, must decide whether with liberty it can achieve loyalty also, completing the fabric which the fathers commenced.

ROBERT C. WINTHROP

*Oration on the centennial anniversary of the Declaration of Independence (Boston, Massachusetts, 1876)**

A scion of an old and prominent Massachusetts family, Winthrop had a long career in state and national politics; he is the great grandfather of Democratic politician John F. Kerry. His very long oration devotes most of its pages to recalling the events of 1776. He emphasizes memorials, including the Statue of Liberty and a proposed statue to Jefferson and Adams.

[T]he name I bear may serve . . . as a link between the earliest settlement of New England, two centuries and a half ago, and the grand culmination of that settlement in this Centennial Epoch of American Independence . . .

. . .

Go back with me, then, for a few moments at least, to that great year of our Lord, and that great day of American Liberty. Transport yourselves with me, in imagination, to Philadelphia. It will require but little effort for any of us

---

* Robert C. Winthrop, *Oration on the centennial anniversary of the Declaration of independence* (John Wilson & Son, 1876).

to do so, for all our hearts are there already. Yes, we are all there,—from the Atlantic to the Pacific, from the Lakes to the Gulf,—we are all there, at this high noon of our Nation's birthday, in that beautiful City of Brotherly Love, rejoicing in all her brilliant displays, and partaking in the full enjoyment of all her pageantry and pride.

. . .

Observe and watch the movements, listen attentively to the words, look steadfastly at the countenances, of the men who compose the little Congress assembled there. Braver, wiser, nobler men have never been gathered and grouped under a single roof, before or since, in any age, on any soil beneath the sun. What are they doing? What are they daring? Who are they, thus to do, and thus to dare?

. . .

[Over the next ten pages, Winthrop gives capsule portraits of members of the Congress and minutely describes their action around the passage of the Declaration. He then turns to a discussion of John Adams and Thomas Jefferson and the extraordinary coincidence that they died on the same day, July 4, 1826, the fiftieth anniversary of the Declaration's proclamation.]

. . .

And now another Fifty Years have passed away, and we are holding our high Centennial Festival; and still that most striking, most impressive, most memorable coincidence in all American history, or even in the authentic records of mankind, is without a visible monument anywhere ! . . . And what could be a worthier or juster commemoration of the marvellous coincidence of which I have just spoken, and of the men who were the subjects of it . . . than . . . a Monument, with the statues of Adams and Jefferson, side by side and hand in hand, upon the same base . . . ! It would be a new tie between Massachusetts and Virginia. It would be a new bond of that Union which is the safety and the glory of both.

. . .

[T]he very nation which counts Voltaire among its greatest celebrities [France] . . . has taken the lead in pointing out the true grounds on which our American Age may challenge and claim a special recognition. An association of Frenchmen, under the lead of some of their most distinguished statesmen and scholars,—has proposed to erect, and is engaged in erecting, as their contribution to our Centennial, a gigantic statue [the Statue of Liberty] at the very throat of the harbor of our supreme commercial emporium [New York City], which shall symbolize the legend inscribed on its pedestal,—"Liberty enlightening the World!"

ACKNOWLEDGMENTS

Thanks go to Brian Distelberg, Alex Cullina, Lara Heimert, and the whole wonderful team at Basic Books for their encouragement and skill in making a manuscript into a book. It is a pleasure and honor to work with them. My great appreciation, as ever, to Jennifer Lyons, my agent, who fights for my projects and always believes.

I am very grateful to colleagues and friends who generously read the manuscript and gave me feedback. David Henkin, David Waldstreicher, Mark Lilla, James E. Lewis Jr., Claire Parfait, Peter Mancall, Larry Glickman, and Peter Wirzbicki all offered trenchant comments that helped me say what I meant—and say it better. Scott Heerman worked his magic on the whole shebang. Michael Blaakman answered a key question. Conversations with Quentin Deluermoz and Clément Thibaud helped sharpen my methods.

It was a pleasure to discuss the book at the Omohundro Institute's Annual Conference, at the École des Hautes Études en Sciences Sociales, and at RéDEHJA's Jeune Amérique seminar. I am also grateful to the institutions that provided time and space to research and write this book: the USC Dornsife Dean's Office, the National Endowment for the Humanities, Mondes Américains and the École des Hautes Études en Sciences Sociales, and the Minda de Gunzburg Center for European Studies at Harvard.

For research assistance, my thanks go to Scott Wagner and Jonah Rosenthal. Their excellent work added significantly to my understanding of the orations and their contexts.

As always, my family was the heart of the affair. My parents, Jed Perl and Deborah Rosenthal, read an early version and offered excellent advice. Suzanne Perl-Marglin didn't get her way about the title—*The Fourth of July Book* it isn't—but hopefully that won't keep her from reading it. Emmanuelle Marglin-Rosenthal gave me excellent suggestions about the illustrations. Frédérique Apffel-Marglin and Steve Marglin were always game to hear about my latest finds.

Jessica Marglin read the manuscript with her unfailing finesse, delivered more than one pep talk, and gave me precious time to read and write. I'm grateful for the adventure of our life together.

NOTES

In the notes, Fourth of July orations published as separate pamphlets are cited using a nonstandard style: the orator's name, followed by the name of the town and state or territory (in parentheses) *in which the speech was delivered*, followed by the year it was given, then the page number. So "Frederick Douglass, Rochester (NY), 1852, 2" is a citation to page 2 of the Fourth of July oration delivered by Frederick Douglass in Rochester, New York, in 1852. This citation format provides ready access to essential information—namely, the place in which the oration was delivered—that would be missing or difficult to find in a more traditional citation format. Unless otherwise noted, citations refer to the first edition of an oration.

Fourth of July orations that were published in newspapers, or which I used in other formats than a printed pamphlet, are cited using the standard style.

The *Fourth of July Orations Database* is mentioned a number of times. This database is available at http://www.julyfourthorations.org. It includes entries for each of the unique Fourth of July orations published in pamphlet form that I and my assistants identified for the period 1777–1876. (Sources included, but were not limited to, the Evans, Shaw/Shoemaker, and Sabin bibliographies; the Harvard

Libraries catalog; the New York State Library catalog; and Worldcat.) The database includes full citations for each oration as well as additional information, such as the total number of pages.

Unless necessary for clarity, citations to books include the name of the publisher but not the place of publication.

Introduction. Forget 1776

1. Robert Pettus Hay, "Freedom's Jubilee: One Hundred Years of the Fourth of July, 1776–1876" (PhD diss., University of Kentucky, 1967), 15–17.
2. L. H. Butterfield et al., eds., *Diary and Autobiography of John Adams*, 4 vols. (Belknap Press of Harvard University Press, 1961), 2:173–175; Francis S. Drake, *The Town of Roxbury: Its Memorable Persons and Places* (Municipal Printing Office, 1908), 421–422.
3. William Gordon, Boston (MA), 1777, 22, 23–26, 34, n.p.
4. Numbers of orations: See Charles Francis Adams, Quincy (MA), 1869, 4 (a "moderate" estimate). Quotation: Thomas U. P. Charlton, Savannah (GA), 1802, 4. See also Samuel Taggart, Colrain (MA), 1803, n.p. and 22, who noted that "on account of the extreme length of the performance, a few passages were omitted in the delivery" of his orations. He restored them in the publication and added a footnote responding to news that had arrived since the oration was delivered. The *Fourth of July Oration Database* includes nearly 2,500 unique items for the period 1777–1876.
5. For excellent discussions of Fourth of July celebrations in partisan context, see David Waldstreicher, *In the Midst of Perpetual Fetes: The Making of American Nationalism, 1776–1820* (University of North Carolina Press, 1997), esp. 80–83, 137–138, 216–230; and Simon P. Newman, *Parades and the Politics of the Street: Festive Culture in the Early American Republic* (University of Pennsylvania Press, 1997), 83–119. In some of the first Boston celebrations, the orations came first. In Portsmouth,

New Hampshire, in 1782, there was a meal first, then a procession and an oration. See Howard Hastings Martin, "Orations on the Anniversary of American Independence, 1777–1876" (PhD diss., Northwestern University, 1955), 19–20, 22; Hay, "Freedom's Jubilee," 95–98; and John Bisbe, Southbridge (MA), 1821, 25–28, for a contemporary account.

6. For discussions of ritual in the context of the Fourth, see Waldstreicher, *In the Midst*, 11; and Andrew W. Robertson, "'Look on This Picture . . . And on This!' Nationalism, Localism, and Partisan Images of Otherness in the United States, 1787–1820," *American Historical Review* 106:4 (Oct. 2001): 1267. On ritual reenactment, see Mircea Eliade, *Myth and Reality*, trans. Willard R. Trask (Harper & Row, 1963), 19–20. The Declaration was a kind of legal document—the "title-deed of our liberties," as one orator called it—whose words had to be reproduced exactly in order to affirm their legal force: See Thomas Starr King, Boston (MA), 1852, 6; and John R. Warner, Gettysburg (PA), 1861, 6. For the sense of reenactment, see, e.g., Horace Mann, Dedham (MA), 1823, 4; Bradford Sumner, Boston (MA), 1828, 28, who imagined the "leading spirits" of the Revolution hovering around them; and James S. Allan, Danville (KY), 1835 ("we enter into communion with the departed").

7. Henry D. Gilpin, Philadelphia (PA), 1834, 7; William Slade, Bridport (VT), 1829, 4. Orators used newspapers, government documents, political books and tracts, correspondence, and historical scholarship to create their stories: See, for instance, the citations to Barruel in David Edmond, Ridgefield (CT), 1799, 7; or those to Buffon in Austin Denny, Worcester (MA), 1818, 7. See also Edward Everett, Beverly (MA), 1835, 6–7; Mandrillon cited in Alexander Macwhorter, Newark (NJ), 1794; Charles H. Lyon, Tarrytown (NY), 1839, citing Henry Lord Brougham; William Lloyd Garrison, Boston (MA), 1829, citing Henry Adams; and the laundry list of citations in Giles Bacon Kellogg, Williamstown (MA), 1829, 22. Where possible, I have used details about how these orations were performed to guide my reading of the

texts. On the Massacre orations, see Eric Hinderaker, *Boston's Massacre* (Harvard University Press, 2017), 236–238, 244–255. On jeremiad, see Sacvan Bercovitch, *The American Jeremiad* (University of Wisconsin Press, 2012 [1978]), 6–17, and the works he discusses.

8. George Buchanan, Baltimore (MD), 1791, 17; Charles Hadduck, Lebanon (NH), 1842, 23; William Everett, Boston (MA), 1870, 12–13. Much scholarship has treated the American Revolution from the 1790s on as a question of memory. This includes the classic Michael Kammen, *A Season of Youth: The American Revolution and the Historical Imagination* (Knopf, 1978); and Alfred F. Young, *The Shoemaker and the Tea Party: Memory and the American Revolution* (Beacon Press, 1999), as well as more recent additions, including Michael A. McDonnell et al., eds., *Remembering the Revolution: Memory, History, and Nation Making from Independence to the Civil War* (University of Massachusetts Press, 2013); and Michael D. Hattem, *The Memory of '76: The Revolution in American History* (Yale University Press, 2024). On permanent revolution, though I do not fully agree with either, see Reinhart Koselleck, *Futures Past: On the Semantics of Historical Time* (MIT Press, 1985), 49–51; and Dan Edelstein, *The Revolution to Come: A History of an Idea from Thucydides to Lenin* (Princeton University Press, 2025), 254–262. The idea of the American Revolution-in-progress was not universal. See, e.g., William Emerson, Boston (MA), 1802, 14 ("gloriously terminated"); Samuel Adams Wells, Boston (MA), 1819, 3; Edward Everett, Charlestown (MA), 1828, 35; and Charles Hammond, Mashpaug (CT), 1853, 3.
9. Samuel Knapp, Newburyport (MA), 1810, 13; Oliver Cobb, Rochester (MA), 1803, 8–9.
10. John S. Farmer, *Americanisms Old and New: A Dictionary of Words, Phrases and Colloquialisms Peculiar to the United States* . . . (Poulter & Sons, 1889), 509; Austin Denny, Worcester (MA), 1818, 11.
11. The *Fourth of July Orations Database* includes 2,279 orations through 1875: The average is 23.7 orations per year, ranging

from a low of 1 to a high of 57. In addition to the important studies by Waldstreicher, *In the Midst*, and Newman, *Parades*, there have been several dissertations on the Fourth of July orations: Hay, "Freedom's Jubilee"; Martin, "Orations"; and Stephen Elliot James, "The Other Fourth of July: The Meanings of Black Identity at American Celebrations of Independence, 1770–1863" (PhD diss., Harvard, 1997). See also Len Travers, *Celebrating the Fourth: Independence Day and the Rites of Nationalism in the Early Republic* (University of Massachusetts Press, 1999). Though they are not framed as studies of the orations, Gordon S. Wood, *The Creation of the American Republic, 1776–1787* (University of North Carolina Press for the Institute of Early American History and Culture, 1969) and Paul C. Nagel, *This Sacred Trust: American Nationality 1778–1898* (Oxford University Press, 1971) both use the orations extensively.

12. Isaac Bourdeaux, Charleston (SC), 1803, 4, 20. See, for instance, the prefatory note to P. H. Wendover's 1806 oration, delivered in New York City: The "General Committee of Arrangements . . . have directed us . . . to return you thanks for your Oration . . . and request of you the favour of a copy for publication." P. H. Wendover, New York (NY), 1806, n.p. This conceit was sometimes put to the lie by disagreements about the choice of an orator, for which see the account of dissention in Nottingham West, NH, in *The Republican Sentiment of New-Hampshire* (1828), 28. On "spokespeople," see E. P. Thompson, *The Making of the English Working Class* (Pantheon, 1963), ch. 15, esp. 631–642; Pierre Bourdieu, *Distinction: A Social Critique of the Judgement of Taste*, trans. Richard Nice (Harvard University Press, 1984), ch. 7; Quentin Deluermoz, *Commune(s) 1870–1871. Une traversée des mondes au XIXe siècle* (Seuil, 2020), esp. 300–307; and Gareth Stedman Jones, "Rethinking Chartism," in *Languages of Class* (Cambridge University Press, 1984), esp. 93–102, which articulates the case for intellectual histories of social movements.
13. Of 213 orations in the *Fourth of July Orations Database* in the period 1777–1800, 146 (68.5 percent) were delivered in MA

(including ME), CT, NH, RI, or VT. For a concise statement of New England's socioeconomic distinctiveness in the period, see Charles Sellers, *The Market Revolution: Jacksonian America, 1815–1846* (Oxford University Press, 1991), 18–19.

14. See Robert A. Gross and Mary Kelley, eds., *A History of the Book in America, vol. 2, An Extensive Republic: Print, Culture, and Society in the New Nation, 1790–1840* (University of North Carolina Press, 2010), esp. 94, 120, 123–125; and "Introduction" in Scott E. Casper et al., eds., *A History of the Book in America, Volume 3: The Industrial Book, 1840–1880* (University of North Carolina Press, 2007), esp. 5–9.

Chapter 1. Place and Time

1. Alexander C. Macwhorter, Newark (NJ), 1794, n.p., 7–8.
2. I am here in firm agreement with Mark Peterson, *The City-State of Boston: The Rise and Fall of an Atlantic Power, 1630–1865* (Princeton University Press, 2019), 629–632.
3. For parallel discussions of origin points and chronologies in other American cultures see, esp., Rebecca Earle, "'Padres de La Patria' and the Ancestral Past: Commemorations of Independence in Nineteenth-Century Spanish America," *Journal of Latin American Studies* 34:4 (Nov. 2002): 775–805; and Enrique Plasencia de la Parra, "La visión de la independencia a través de los discursos conmemorativos. (1825–1867)" (PhD diss., UNAM, 1989).
4. William Jones, Concord (MA), 1794, 15.
5. Robert Barnwell, Beaufort (SC), 1803, 17; see the similar language in Francis Blake, Worcester (MA), 1796, 11–12.
6. See Robert Middlekauff, *The Glorious Cause: The American Revolution, 1763–1789* (Oxford University Press, 1982), 611–621; Allan Kulikoff, "'Such Things Ought Not to Be': The American Revolution and the First National Great Depression," in *The World of the Revolutionary American Republic: Land, Labor, and the Conflict for a Continent*, ed. Andrew Shankman (Routledge, 2014), esp. 135, 147–151; and Terry Bouton, *"The People," the Founders, and the Troubled Ending of the American Revolution* (Oxford University Press, 2009), ch. 7. On the American

Revolution as civil war, see esp. Holger Hoock, *Scars of Independence: America's Violent Birth* (Crown, 2017); and Alan Taylor, *American Revolutions: A Continental History, 1750–1804* (W. W. Norton, 2016), ch. 6, esp. 211–213.

7. Rise of parties in Congress: Noble E. Cunningham, *The Jeffersonian Republicans: The Formation of Party Organization, 1789–1801* (University of North Carolina Press for the Institute of Early American History and Culture, 1957), 68–76. Ideologies of the parties: Stanley Elkins and Eric McKitrick, *The Age of Federalism* (Oxford University Press, 1993), 112–131; Sean Wilentz, *The Rise of American Democracy: Jefferson to Lincoln* (W. W. Norton, 2005), 42–49; Alan Taylor, *American Republics: A Continental History of the United States, 1783–1850* (W. W. Norton, 2021), 47–51; Linda K. Kerber, *Federalists in Dissent: Imagery and Ideology in Jeffersonian America* (Cornell University Press, 1970), 27–59.
8. See Cunningham, *Jeffersonian Republicans*, 116–128; and Wilentz, *Rise*, 75, 83–98, 100–125.
9. Jonathan Grout, Heath (MA), 1803, i. Local committee: See, e.g., Nathaniel Scudder Prime, Cambridge (NY), 1825, n.p. On local recruitment, see, e.g., Elisha Bartlett, Lowell (MA), 1848, and orations cited below. Most orations do not offer this type of detail on the ceremony or the performance of the oration.
10. John Cushing, Ashburnham (MA), 1796, 3; Joseph Blake, Boston (MA), 1792, 4; William Loughton Smith, Charleston (SC), 1796, 4. For vivid later examples, see James Trecothick Austin, Boston (MA), 1829, 6 ("Massachusetts is the mother of the Revolution"); Asa Dodge Smith, Weston (VT), 1853; Charles Hammond, Mashpaug (CT), 1853, 18; and George R. Parburt, *Sylph* (at sea), 1849, 21–24 (identifying the home towns of each member of the audience).
11. John McKnight, New York (NY), 1794, 13–15. Edward Everett, Charlestown (MA), 1828, 6, argued that "the free [people] of all climes and nations, are themselves a people."
12. Edward Gray, Boston (MA), 1790, 12, 13–14. Note that these last phrases were pronounced by Gray in a negative sense about

the Greek city-states; they were absent from them. The Constitution, in his view, fixed these absences that had so damaged the Greek case. For his political leanings, see David Waldstreicher, *In the Midst of Perpetual Fetes: The Making of American Nationalism, 1776–1820* (University of North Carolina Press, 1997), 108.

13. Oliver Cobb, Rochester (MA), 1803, 8; Jerome Van Crowinshield Smith, South Boston (MA), 1835, 41–42. See also Andrew Dunlap, Salem (MA), 1819, 5; Silas Pinckney Holbrook, Medfield (MA), 1822; and the elaborate "tree of liberty" metaphor in J. P. C. Sampson, Litchfield (CT), 1818, 10. For a discussion of "germ theories" in history, see Daniel Lord Smail, *On Deep History and the Brain* (University of California Press, 2007), 76–81.
14. William Jones, Concord (MA), 1794, 19. Caleb Cushing, Newburyport (MA), 1821, esp. 5–6 and 16–18, also paired the local with the global.
15. Thomas Allen, Pittsfield (MA), 1803; Estes Howe, Worcester (MA), 1808, 14. Charles Perkins, Norwich (CT), 1822, 23, criticized "indifference" to the ongoing servitude of "other nations." Joshua S. Henshaw, Utica (NY), 1848, 10–11, said that Americans were necessarily "concerned" in the struggles "by the people of the several states of Europe."
16. Francis Blake, Worcester (MA), 1796, 1; Joshua Heywood, Amherst (MA), 1796, 12. See also B. F. Bailey, Burlington (VT), 1828, 6–8.
17. Timothy Hilliard, Portland (ME), 13–16.
18. Oliver Cobb, Rochester (MA), 1803, 8–9. Mary Hall Leonard, *Mattapoisett and Old Rochester, Massachusetts* (The Grafton Press, 1907), 88.
19. Samuel Bugbee, Wrentham (MA), 1803, 5–7; Robert Young Hayne, Charleston (SC), 1814, 23. See also the discussion of Spanish liberalism in Charles Curtis Pelham, Boston (MA), 1823, 24–26; and Horace Mann, Dedham (MA), 1823, 18–19.
20. See Patrick Griffin and Frank Cogliano, eds., *Ireland and America: Empire, Revolution, and Sovereignty* (University of Virginia Press, 2021); Andrew Jackson O'Shaughnessy, *An Empire*

Divided: The American Revolution and the British Caribbean (University of Pennsylvania Press, 2000); and Joseph Chandler, Monmouth (ME), 1806, 11. See also Edwin A. White, Worcester (MA), 1814, 16; and Charles Pelham Curtis, Boston (MA), 1823, 11–18 (a counterfactual history imagining if the British had won the Revolutionary War).

21. Benjamin Gleason, Providence (RI), 1802, 3. See also Nehemia Cleaveland, Newburyport (MA), 1824, 4.
22. See Nathan Perl-Rosenthal, "Ideas of Revolution in the Age of Atlantic Revolutions," *Modern Intellectual History* (2023), esp. 1013–1017; and Levi Hubbell, Albany (NY), 1835, 10.
23. Mercy Otis Warren, *History of the Rise, Progress, and Termination of the American Revolution* (Manning & Loring, 1805), 1:27; David Ramsay, *The History of the American Revolution* (Aitken, 1789), 1:42–43.
24. Elijah Kellogg, Portland (ME), 1795, 6–8. Wilmot Brookings Mitchell, ed., *Elijah Kellogg: The Man and His Work* (Lee and Shepard, 1903), 3–4.
25. Elijah Kellogg, Portland (ME), 1795, 9–10. A similar short chronology was used by Daniel Dewey Barnard, Albany (NY), 1835, 33, who denied a British genealogy for American liberty, and by Samuel Bryant, West Dedham (MA), 1839, 4.
26. Elijah Kellogg, Portland (ME), 12–13.
27. John Phillips, Boston (MA), 1794, 5–8; Joseph Chandler, Monmouth (ME), 1806, 5–8. Albert Gorton Greene, Providence (RI), 1823, 8, saw the "art of printing" as the origin point of American liberty. George Washington Adams, Quincy (MA), 1823, started with the rise of Christianity.
28. Isaac Watts Crane, Newark (NJ), 1797, 3–4; Paul Allen, Rehoboth (MA), 1806, 9–10, 12. See also Edward Tyrrel Channing, Boston (MA), 1817, 10–11; and Robert Elfe, Charleston (SC), 1821, 13–14, who argued that "America was destined to be free."
29. Jonathan Loring Austin, Boston (MA), 1786, 6, 12–14; James Spear Loring, *The Hundred Boston Orators Appointed by the Municipal Authorities and Other Public Bodies, from 1770 to 1852* (Jewett & Co., 1854), 179–180.

30. Joel Barlow, Hartford (CT), 1787, 8, 11; Samuel Deane, Portland (ME), 1793, 11–12; Josiah Quincy, Boston (MA), 1798 [2nd ed.], 16.
31. William Linn, New York (NY), 1791, 33–34; John Champlin Thompson, Burlington (VT), 1828, 3. This theme was a frequent one over the decades: see Albert Gorton Greene, Providence (RI), 1823, 15–16; and Simeon Howard Calhoun, Williamstown (MA), 1829, 12.
32. Simon P. Newman, *Parades and the Politics of the Street: Festive Culture in the Early American Republic* (University of Pennsylvania Press, 1997), 94.

Chapter 2. Doubts

1. Samuel Lorenzo Knapp, Newburyport (MA), 1810, 15, 8–9.
2. John Geddes Jr., Charleston (SC), 1821, 14. This was still a concern for Charles H. Lyon, Tarrytown (NY), 1839, 12–13.
3. Enos Hitchcock, Providence (RI), 1788, 9; Joseph Blake Jr., Boston (MA), 1792, 7. See also Stephen Thacher, Kennebunk (ME), 1803, 13.
4. Theodore Dwight, Hartford (CT), 1792, 11–12; John Quincy Adams, Boston (MA), 1793, 17; Enos Hitchcock, Providence (RI), 1793, 19; Samuel Deane, Portland (ME), 1793, 12; Josiah Quincy, Boston (MA), 1798, 16.
5. Josiah Henderson, Stephen-Town [Westchester] (NY), 1803, 20–21; John Crane, Douglas (MA), 1802, 9, 19.
6. Rollin Carolus Mallary, Poultney (VT), 1814, 7. See also similar language from Robert Young Hayne, Charleston (SC), 1814, 6: "The United States of America, is the only free country on earth"; Edwin A. White, Worcester (MA), 1814, 9; and John Holmes, Alfred (ME), 1815, 17. Though see, by contrast, the triumphant tone of G. W. Ridgely, Lexington (KY), 1822, in *Masonic Miscellany and Ladies' Literary Magazine* 2:65.
7. Joseph Blake Jr., Boston (MA), 1792. The theme was still alive and kicking nearly six decades later in the orations by Robert Raikes Raymond, Hamilton (NY), 1848, 15, and Thomas Starr King, Boston (MA), 1852, 19–21.

8. Barbara B. Oberg et al., eds., *The Papers of Thomas Jefferson: Main Series* (Princeton University Press, 1950–2023), 33:149. The word had already been used by George Washington in his first inaugural address, but it did not make a similar impression.
9. In general, see Steven Shapin, *A Social History of Truth: Civility and Science in Seventeenth-Century England* (University of Chicago Press, 1994); and Simon Schaffer and Steven Shapin, *Leviathan and the Air-Pump: Hobbes, Boyle, and the Experimental Life* (Princeton University Press, 1985). On North Americans' reception of this discourse, see James Delbourgo, *A Most Amazing Scene of Wonders: Electricity and Enlightenment in Early America* (Harvard University Press, 2006), esp. 23–24.
10. Shapin, *A Social History of Truth*, 247–266; Schaffer and Shapin, *Leviathan and the Air-Pump*, 3–7, 23–49.
11. William Cunningham, Fitchburg (MA), 1803, 12; William Slade, Bridport (VT), 1829, 12; Edwin Forrest, New York (NY), 1838, 12. See also Samuel Austin, Newport (RI), 1822, 14. In Hilda Sabato, *Republics of the New World: The Revolutionary Political Experiment in Nineteenth-Century Latin America* (Princeton University Press, 2018), 2, 9, 209, Sabato uses "experiment" systematically, but it is her term, not that of the historical actors themselves. "Experiment" was never, to my knowledge, used by French republicans to characterize any of the French Republics. Interestingly, however, William W. Greenough, Boston (MA), 1849, 17, extended the language to the French Revolution, which he called a "French experiment."
12. "Self government": Simeon Howard Calhoun, Williamstown (MA), 1829, 7; B. F. Bailey, Burlington (VT), 1828, 15; Henry James, Newport (RI), 1861, 22; Horace Mann, Boston (MA), 1842, 2; William Cunningham, Fitchburg (MA), 1803, 12; "Mr Blake" in John Davis, Worcester (MA), 1816, 23. See also George C. Wilde, Newburyport (MA), 1823, 4.
13. Edward Tyrrel Channing, Boston (MA), 1817, 17; George C. Wilde, Newburyport (MA), 1823, 4. See also Eric Foner, *The Story of American Freedom* (W. W. Norton, 1998), xiv–xx.

14. James S. Allan, Danville (KY), 1835, 12; George Bancroft, Northampton (MA), 1826, 13. Henry Barney Smith, Dorchester (MA), 1822, 10–11, thought the gradual accumulation of political "experience" would enable future generations to "perfect" the government.
15. John Quincy Adams, Quincy (MA), 1831, 28; Joseph M. Corr, Philadelphia (PA), 1834, in Dorothy Porter, ed., *Early Negro Writing, 1760–1837* (Black Classic Press, 1995), 152; John Appleton, Portland (ME), 1838, 11. See also Henry Bailey, Charleston (SC), 1836, 9 ("the revolution was not the charlatanerie of a lucky experiment"); and Nelson Mitchell, Charleston (SC), 1848, 23 ("wild experiment"). Samuel Osgood, Nashua (NH), 1839, 11, rejected the language of experiment altogether.
16. Alexander Brown, Pittsburgh (PA), 1842, 23; Horace Mann, Boston (MA), 1842, 4. Many orators shared this doubting tone: George C. Wilde, Newburyport (MA), 1823, 14.
17. Data from the *Fourth of July Orations Database*. Alexander C. Macwhorter, Newark (NJ), 1794, 16. Caleb Cushing, Newburyport (MA), 1821, 4, said he had "chosen for [his] topic the revolutionary convulsions, which are at the present time agitating the whole of Europe." See also Henry Barney Smith, Dorchester (MA), 1822, 14–17.
18. Samuel Brazer Jr., Lancaster (MA), 1806, 8–9; Nathaniel Cogswell, Newburyport (MA), 1808, 5–6; Noah Bisbee Jr., Richmond (NH), 1806, 19; Joseph Clark, Rochester (NH), 1794, 10; Richard White, *The Middle Ground: Indians, Empires, and Republics in the Great Lakes Region, 1650–1815* (Cambridge University Press, 1991), chs. 10–11; Ned Blackhawk, *The Rediscovery of America: Native Peoples and the Unmaking of U.S. History* (Yale University Press, 2023), ch. 7; Brian DeLay, "The Arms Trade and American Revolutions," *American Historical Review* 128:3 (Sept. 2023): 1144–1181.
19. David Daggett, New Haven (CT), 1787, 4; Samuel Elliot, West Springfield (MA), 1803, 23 (quotation); Robert Barnwell, Beaufort (SC), 1803, 9–10; B. F. Bailey, Burlington (VT), 1828, 11. Eliminationist rhetoric: see also William Morse, Nantucket

(MA), 1829, 4–5. See Philip Deloria, *Playing Indian* (Yale University Press, 1998), esp. 48–54.

20. On Polybius, see Dan Edelstein, *The Revolution to Come: A History of an Idea from Thucydides to Lenin* (Princeton University Press, 2025), 47–59.
21. This and previous paragraph: J. G. A. Pocock, *The Machiavellian Moment: Florentine Political Thought and the Atlantic Republican Tradition* (Princeton University Press, 1975); Martin van Gelderen and Quentin Skinner, eds., *Republicanism: A Shared European Heritage*, 2 vols. (Cambridge University Press, 2002); but see also David Wootton, ed., *Republicanism, Liberty, and Commercial Society, 1649–1776* (Stanford University Press, 1994); and the trenchant critique by Daniel T. Rodgers, "Republicanism: The Career of a Concept," *Journal of American History* 79:1 (June 1992): 11–38.
22. Caroline Robbins, *The Eighteenth-Century Commonwealthman* (Harvard University Press, 1959); Bernard Bailyn, *The Ideological Origins of the American Revolution* (Belknap Press of Harvard University Press, 1967); Eran Shalev, *Rome Reborn on Western Shores: Historical Imagination and the Creation of the American Republic* (University of Virginia Press, 2009); and Gordon S. Wood, *The Creation of the American Republic, 1776–1787* (University of North Carolina Press for the Institute of Early American History and Culture, 1969).
23. Henry Bailey, Charleston (SC), 1836, 5. On the transition to kingless government, see Nathan R. Perl-Rosenthal, "The 'Divine Right of Republics': Hebraic Republicanism and the Debate over Kingless Government in Revolutionary America," *William and Mary Quarterly* 66:3 (July 2009): 535–564.
24. See Silas Pinckney Holbrook, Medfield (MA), 1822, 14. The oration by John Morin Scott, Easton (PA), 1834, was almost entirely about the Marquis de Lafayette, including a long discussion of his role in the American Revolution.
25. Francis Blake, Worcester (MA), 16–17; Alexander C. Macwhorter, Newark (NJ), 1794, 17–18.
26. Archibald Buchanan, Baltimore (MD), 1794, 38–39; Joseph Clark, Rochester (NH), 1794, 5–6. Edward C. Papenfuse, *In Pursuit of*

Profit: The Annapolis Merchants in the Era of the American Revolution, 1763–1805 (Johns Hopkins University Press, 1975), 112.

27. Josiah Quincy, Boston (MA), 1798, 17; John Lathrop Jr., Boston (MA), 1796, 22; George Bancroft, Northampton (MA), 1826, 7–10. Some orators expressed suspicion about revolution altogether—see Pliny Merrick, Worcester (MA), 1817, 15—or took a more equivocal view of Napoleon, as did John Morin Scott, Easton (PA), 1834, 19–22.
28. Jonathan Ellis, Brunswick (ME), 1806, 7. This was a common theme: see Richard Henry Dana, Cambridge (MA), 1814, 14; and Hugh Swinton Legaré, Charleston (SC), 1823, in Mary Swinton Legaré, ed., *Writings of Hugh Swinton Legaré* (Burges & James, 1846), 1:260–262.
29. On the republican revolutions and their ideologies, see Sabato, *Republics of the New World*; Anthony McFarlane, *War and Independence in Spanish America* (Routledge, 2014); José Antonio Aguilar and Rafael Rojas, eds., *El republicanismo en Hispanoamérica: Ensayos de historia intelectual y política* (Fondo de Cultura Económica, 2016), esp. chs. 2, 3, 6; and Gabriel Entin, *En quête de république: Une histoire de la communauté politique en Amérique hispanique* (Presses universitaires de Rennes, 2025), ch. 6.
30. Leonard M. Parker, Charlestown (MA), 1816, 15; Gerry Fairbanks, Boston (MA), 1821, 19, 16. See also J. P. C. Sampson, Litchfield (CT), 1818, 12, who complained that Americans were not sufficiently sympathetic to the South Americans; Nehemia Cleaveland, Newburyport (MA), 1824, 15 ("thought abroad to his struggling brethren in the cause of liberty"); Henry V. S. Vanden Bergh, Stillwater (NY), 1824, 14–16, worrying about a transatlantic plot against liberty; and Bradford Sumner, Boston (MA), 1828, 13–16.
31. On varying attitudes toward the South American revolutions, see esp. Caitlin Fitz, *Our Sister Republics: The United States in an Age of American Revolutions* (W. W. Norton, 2016), esp. 125–134, 232–239.

32. For the Greek Revolution, see Solomon Lincoln Jr., Hingham (MA), 1826, 20–22; Edward Everett, Charlestown (MA), 1828, 37–38; William Morse, Nantucket (MA), 1829, 15. For others, see Francis Baylies, Taunton (MA), 1831, 7–22; Henry Bailey, Charleston (SC), 1836, 13–15; and Francis Lieber, Greenville (SC), 1851, 2–4, 12. My interpretation of these comparisons is the opposite of David Waldstreicher, *In the Midst of Perpetual Fetes: The Making of American Nationalism, 1776–1820* (University of North Carolina Press, 1997), 296.
33. Orville Luther Holley, Lyons (NY), 1822, 10, 17. See also the mention of Haiti in John Bisbe, Southbridge (MA), 1821, 21, and Nathaniel Bouton, Concord (NH), 1825, 20.
34. Orville Luther Holley, Lyons (NY), 1822, 15.
35. Orville Luther Holley, Lyons (NY), 1822, 19.
36. John Lathrop Jr., Boston (MA), 1796, 12; Isaac Bourdeaux, Charleston (SC), 1803, 4.
37. William Hobby, Augusta (GA), 1799, 7; Hooper Cumming, New York (NY), 1824, 4.
38. Nathaniel Cogswell, Newburyport (MA), 4; Noah Bodman, Massachusetts, 1803. Here are a handful of other examples, out of many: Henry V. S. Vander Bergh, Stillwater (NY), 1824, 6–8; William Drayton, Charleston (SC), 1831, 7; and Edward Everett, Beverly (MA), 1835, 17–48.
39. Isaac Bourdeaux, Charleston (SC), 1803, 24.
40. David Augustus Leonard, Dighton (MA), 1803, 23.
41. Robert Barnwell, Beaufort (SC), 1803, 29. On the life expectancy of the era, see Philip J. Greven, *Four Generations: Population, Land, and Family in Colonial Andover, Massachusetts* (Cornell University Press, 1970), 193–194; and Herbert S. Klein, *A Population History of the United States* (Cambridge University Press, 2004), 101–110.
42. Hooper Cumming, Schenectady (NY), 1821, 11; Andrew Dunlap, Salem (MA), 1819, 7; Gad Hitchcock, Hanson (MA), 1829, 7; Solomon Lincoln Jr., Hingham (MA), 1826, 10. See also B. F. Bailey, Burlington (VT), 1828, 18. See T. T. Bouvé et al., *History*

of the Town of Hingham, Massachusetts* (By the Town, 1893), 1:214.

43. See John P. Resch, *Suffering Soldiers: Revolutionary War Veterans, Moral Sentiment, and Political Culture in the Early Republic* (University of Massachusetts Press, 1999), esp. 218.
44. John Holmes, Alfred (ME), 1815, 6. See also Joseph Richardson, Weymouth (MA), 1828, 22, which expressed similar sentiments.
45. David Ramsay, Charleston (SC), 1820, 23. See also William Plumer, Portsmouth (NH), 1828, 22; and Nathaniel Loring, Charlestown (MA), 1822, 6: "The present generation is the commencement of a new order of things." Nathaniel Bowen, Providence (RI), 1802, 18.
46. Andrew Dunlap, Salem (MA), 1819, 4.

Chapter 3. Enemies Within

1. See *The Commemorative Services of the First Parish in Hingham on the Two Hundredth Anniversary of the Building of Its Meeting-House* (Hingham, 1882), 147–148.
2. James Humphrey Wilder, Hingham (MA), 1832, 12, 8, 19.
3. James Davis Knowles, Boston (MA), 1828, 4, 10–17; Peleg Whitman Chandler, Boston (MA), 1844, 13. Horace Mann, Dedham (MA), 1823, 5–9, attacked hereditary authority, the "Feudal System"; Freeman G. Brown, Washington (DC), 1835, 11, similarly urged "responsibility" on newspaper editors. This theme was still being sounded over thirty years later by Charles Daly, New York (NY), 1862, 23.
4. This and the next paragraph: Daniel Walker Howe, *What Hath God Wrought: The Transformation of America, 1815–1848* (Oxford University Press, 2007), chs. 1 and 4; Sven Beckert, *Empire of Cotton: A Global History* (Knopf, 2015), ch. 5; Sellers, *Market Revolution*, chs. 1 and 3.
5. The classic studies include Whitney R. Cross, *The Burned-over District: The Social and Intellectual History of Enthusiastic Religion in Western New York, 1800–1850* (Cornell University Press, 1950); Paul E. Johnson, *A Shopkeeper's Millennium: Society and Revivals in Rochester, New York, 1815–1837* (Hill & Wang, 1978);

and Nathan O. Hatch, *The Democratization of American Christianity* (Yale University Press, 1989). See also Howe, *What Hath*, ch. 5.

6. Benjamin Silliman, New Haven (CT), 1832, 2.
7. Peleg Whitman Chandler, Boston (MA), 1844, 15, 25–27, 14.
8. Peleg Whitman Chandler, Boston (MA), 1844, 49, 24. Very similar language was used by Edmund B. Fairfield, Hillsdale (MI), 1853, 4: "A nation . . . is simply the aggregate of the individuals composing it."
9. William H. Fondey, Albany (NY), 1838, 10–11. See also George Sullivan, Boston (MA), 1816, 11ff.; Edgar Buckingham, Trenton (NJ), 1842, 8–14; and George Washington Doane, Burlington (NJ), 1853, 14–15. Edward Everett, Beverly (MA), 1835, 15. See also Eber Wheaton, New York (NY), 1828, 13, who viewed the War of 1812 as the "triumph of virtue over corruption."
10. On the revolutionary-era background, see Alan Heimert, *Religion and the American Mind: From the Great Awakening to the Revolution* (Harvard University Press, 1966), esp. 481–494. Confessional language increased significantly in orations over time. Out of the 190 orations in the Evans bibliography of American imprints (pre-1800), just 39, or 20 percent, used the word *Christian*. In a sample of 219 digitized orations from 1820 to 1840 [Gale Sabin Americana], 128, or 58 percent, spoke of "Christian[s]." Nathaniel Bouton, Concord (NH), 1825, 5; John Cross Smith, Washington (DC), 1844, 8–9; George S. Wilson, Sackets Harbor (NY), 1839, 5. For later examples, see Isaac N. Shannon, New Brunswick (NJ), 1852, 3–4; and Robert Raikes Raymond, Hamilton (NY), 1848, 38.
11. Charles Brickett Hadduck, Lebanon (NH), 1842, 8, 23; George Washington Bethune, Philadelphia (PA), 1835, 18; Ezra Stiles Ely, Philadelphia (PA), 1827, 7–8, 4, 5, 11–12. On toleration and religious diversity, see the oration by the Catholic John C. Devereaux, Jamaica (NY), 1852, 5–11.
12. Ezra Stiles Ely, Philadelphia (PA), 1842, 11–13, 25; George Washington Bethune, Philadelphia (PA), 1835, 17. Moses Thacher, Augusta (ME), 1832, 6–7, attributed the nation's ills to "Freemasonry."

13. W. J. Rorabaugh, *The Alcoholic Republic: An American Tradition* (Oxford University Press, 1979), 191–202; Samuel J. May, Dryden (NY), 1842, 3, 15–16.
14. Nathaniel Tucker Bent, Raynham (MA), 1842, 4, 10, 18–20. Another example is to be found in the two orations given by Jonathan Kittredge, both in New Hampshire: Jonathan Kittredge, Bath (NH), 1828, and Jonathan Kittredge, Plymouth (NH), 1829.
15. Heman Humphrey, Amherst (MA), 1828, 26, 19–20.
16. The local recruitment of orators was a persistent tradition. In 1851, a New Haven committee invited the New Yorker Hiram Ketchum to address them, and this was mentioned explicitly in his introduction and in the published pamphlet version of his talk: Hiram Ketchum, New Haven (CT), 1851, 5. Addresses to women: see, e.g., David Daggett, New Haven (CT), 1787, 19–20; Samuel Stillman, Boston (MA), 1789, 25–26; Gerry Fairbanks, Boston (MA), 1821, 16; Charles Edward Pickett, Sacramento (CA), 1857, 25–29.
17. See, e.g., Sean Wilentz, *Chants Democratic: New York City & the Rise of the American Working Class, 1788–1850* (Oxford University Press, 1984), 95–96, 245–246.
18. Data and analysis from *Fourth of July Orations Database*.
19. William Emmons, Boston (MA), 1829, 14. Debt was a common theme: see also Gerry Fairbanks, Boston (MA), 1821, 17.
20. William Lloyd Garrison, Boston (MA), 1829, 2–3, 7.
21. Frances Wright, Philadelphia (PA), 1829, 15, 4, 8, 13.
22. Frances Wright, Philadelphia (PA), 1829, 5, 9.
23. Seth Luther, Brooklyn (NY), 1836, 7, 23, 17; William P. Briggs, Burlington (VT), 1829, 5–9. See also Nathaniel Loring, Charleston (MA), 1822, denouncing the "stupid vanity of the rich" who desired "peculiar privileges" and "enjoy their plunder with impunity"; and James Madison Porter, Easton (PA), 1835, 14, which declared that the "preservation" of the "Constitution . . . depend[ed]" on "mechanics."
24. George Washington Bethune, Philadelphia (PA), 1835, 14–15; S. G. Goodrich, Jamaica Plain (MA), 1835, 18–20.

25. Samuel Osgood, Nashua (NH), 1839, 5–6, 18–20, 26.
26. See Benjamin E. Park, *American Zion: A New History of Mormonism* (Liveright, 2024).
27. Sidney Rigdon, Far West (MO), 1838, 7, 5, 12.
28. Edward Dillingham Bangs, Springfield (MA), 1823, 16; Jerome Van Crowinshield Smith, South Boston (MA), 1835, 13–14. This topic would be enduring: see, e.g., George R. Parburt, *Sylph* (at sea), 1849, 10–16; Edmund B. Fairfield, Hillsdale (MI), 1853, 13–14.
29. Orestes Brownson, Dedham (MA), 1834, 9–10, 21. See Patrick W. Carey, *Orestes A. Brownson: American Religious Weathervane* (Wm. B. Eerdmans, 2004), 1–15.
30. Orestes Brownson, Dedham (MA), 1834, 19–22.
31. James B. Shepard, Raleigh (NC), 1839, 9–10; Levi Hubbell, Albany (NY), 1835, 13–18. See also William Ellis, Accomack (VA), 1851, 12.
32. Horace Mann, Boston (MA), 1842, 2, 4, 6.
33. Horace Mann, Boston (MA), 1842, 22, 24. The oration by Black leader Benjamin Crummell in 1844, discussed in Peter Wirzbicki, *Fighting for the Higher Law: Black and White Transcendentalists Against Slavery* (University of Pennsylvania Press, 2021), 23–25, opened similar themes.

Chapter 4. Slavery

1. Sean Wilentz, *The Rise of American Democracy: Jefferson to Lincoln* (W. W. Norton, 2005), 637–667. See, e.g., the extended discussions of the Fugitive Slave Act in Hiram Ketchum, New Haven (CT), 1851, 19–26; John G. Richardson, Lawrence (MA), 1852, 8.
2. Methodology: The sample is of pamphlets tagged as Fourth of July orations in Readex's Early American Imprints, Parts I and II, and Gale's Sabin Americana. I searched for both "slave" and "flave," and used the cumulative figure. The use of the word *slave* could cause both under- and overcounts of references to racial slavery. Eighteenth-century orators used the term *slavery* to refer to political oppression in general. They and other orators also sometimes spoke about slavery without ever using

the word *slave*—as the US Constitution does. However, using a euphemism such as "sable" produces a similar growth curve: 0/190 (0 percent) before 1800, 18/578 (3 percent) from 1801 to 1820, and 136/484 (28 percent) from 1821 to 1840. This suggests that the use of the keyword *slave* reflected an actual increase in the number of orators who discussed racial slavery. Data collected in 2025.

3. See Ira Berlin, *Many Thousands Gone: The First Two Centuries of Slavery in North America* (Belknap Press of Harvard University Press, 1998), 47–59, 228–239; Leslie M. Harris, *In the Shadow of Slavery: African Americans in New York City, 1626–1863* (University of Chicago Press, 2003), 48–49, 61–69; and Margot Minardi, *Making Slavery History: Abolitionism and the Politics of Memory in Massachusetts* (Oxford University Press, 2010), 14–20, 34–40.
4. On the abolition of slavery in New York, and the celebrations on the Fourth in particular, see Harris, *In the Shadow of Slavery*, 121–128; see also Manisha Sinha, *The Slave's Cause: A History of Abolition* (Yale University Press, 2016), 82–83. William Hamilton, New York (NY), 1827, in *Early Negro Writing*, 97, 100–101, 104. John Bisbe, Southbridge (MA), 1821, 21, hoped that slavery in the "South and the West" would be abolished; William Clagett, Portsmouth (NH), 1839, 11–12, emphasized the contrast between North and South. John Jay, though an advocate for abolition, held people in bondage for a substantial part of his life.
5. Elisha Bartlett, Lowell (MA), 1848, 5–8, 29, 37. See also David A. Bokee, Brooklyn (NY), 1851, 11, who argued that slavery was a local institution.
6. See Benjamin Silliman, New Haven (CT), 1832, 4 (Russia); Samuel Harris, Pittsfield (MA), 1852, 7 (comparisons to Russia and Ottomans); George Barstow, San Jose (CA), 1864, 9 (Russia).
7. Elisha Bartlett, Lowell (MA), 1848, 29; Charles Train, Hopkinton (MA), 1823, 19; Nelson Mitchell, Charleston (SC), 1848, 20–25.
8. On colonization, see Sinha, *Slave's Cause*, 161–166, 239–246; Leonard I. Sweet, *Black Images of America, 1784–1870* (W. W.

Norton, 1976), 35–59; and Giles Bacon Kellogg, Williamstown (MA), 1829, 15. See also Wilbur Fisk, Middletown (CT), 1835; Leonard Bacon, New Haven (CT), 1825, 17, 20–21, offered a similar proposal. On Silliman, see Eric Herschthal, *The Science of Abolition: How Slaveholders Became the Enemies of Progress* (Yale University Press, 2021), 132–136.

9. Augustus Woodbury, Lowell (MA), 1855, 30; Edgar Buckingham, Trenton (NY), 1842, 17; Charles Wentworth Upham, Salem (MA), 1842, 45. This worry may help to explain why Solomon Lincoln Jr., Hingham (MA), 1826, 22, was so firmly against "local prejudices" and "geographical distinctions."
10. Joshua G. Wright, Wilmington (NC), 1851, 13, 16; Robert Field Stockton, Elizabethtown (NJ), 1851, 7. For the Deep South, see John L. Manning, Charleston (SC), 1848, 11–12. See also George R. Parburt, *Sylph* (at sea), 1849, 18–19.
11. For an overall narrative in the US, see Sinha, *Slave's Cause*. On early British abolitionism, see Christopher L. Brown, *Moral Capital: Foundations of British Abolitionism* (University of North Carolina Press for the Omohundro Institute of Early American History and Culture, 2006). For a hemispheric perspective, see Robin Blackburn, *The Reckoning: From the Second Slavery to Abolition, 1776–1888* (Verso, 2024).
12. Sinha, *Slave's Cause*, ch. 7. For an example of gradualist argument, see John Kennedy, Philadelphia (PA), 1828, 4–5. On emancipation in the hemisphere, see Yesenia Barragan, *Freedom's Captives: Slavery and Gradual Emancipation on the Colombian Black Pacific* (Cambridge University Press, 2021).
13. For recent contributions to the long-running debate on this question, see David Waldstreicher, *Slavery's Constitution: From Revolution to Ratification* (Hill & Wang, 2009) and Sean Wilentz, *No Property in Man: Slavery and Antislavery at the Nation's Founding* (Harvard University Press, 2019).
14. Adin Ballou, Westminster (MA), 1843, 4.
15. William Claggett, Portsmouth (NH), 1839, 12; William Lloyd Garrison, South Scituate (MA), 1839, 17; William Lloyd Garrison, Boston (MA), 1838, 7.

16. Joseph M. Corr, Philadelphia (PA), 1834, in *Early Negro Writings*, 147, 151–152; William Lloyd Garrison, Boston (MA), 1829, 5–6.
17. Edwin Pitt Atlee, Philadelphia (PA), 1833, 9, 13–14. Sinha, *Slave's Cause*, 225.
18. Nathaniel Scudder Prime, Cambridge (NY), 1825, 23–24.
19. Edgar Buckingham, Trenton (NY), 1842, 17–18; William Lloyd Garrison, Scituate (MA), 1839, 5–6.
20. The Fifth is discussed in Benjamin Quarles, *Black Abolitionists* (Oxford University Press, 1969), 119–123; and Detine L. Bowers, "A *Strange* Speech of an Estranged People" (PhD diss., Purdue, 1992), 170–197. See also Jonathan Lande, "'Lighting Up the Path of Liberty and Justice': Black Abolitionist Fourth of July Celebrations and the Promise of America from the Fugitive Slave Act to the Civil War," *Journal of African American History* 105:3 (Summer 2020): 364–395.
21. Jeffrey R. Kerr-Ritchie, *Rites of August First: Emancipation Day in the Black Atlantic World* (Louisiana State University Press, 2007), ch. 3; Bowers, "*Strange* Speech," 198ff; Quarles, *Black Abolitionists*, 124–129. See also the perceptive discussion in W. Caleb McDaniel, "The Fourth and the First: Abolitionist Holidays, Respectability, and Radical Interracial Reform," *American Quarterly* 57:1 (Mar. 2005): 133–135, 138–142.
22. David W. Blight, *Frederick Douglass: Prophet of Freedom* (Simon & Schuster, 2018) is the definitive biography. For details of his escape, see Frederick Douglass, *Narrative of the Life of Frederick Douglass, an American Slave* (Anti-Slavery Office, 1845).
23. The scholarship on this speech is vast; see works cited above. James A. Colaiaco, *Frederick Douglass and the Fourth of July* (Macmillan, 2024), is an entire book on the speech, though unfortunately misapprehends the Fourth (see pp. 1–2). The speech was included in the HBO documentary *Frederick Douglass: In Five Speeches* (2022).
24. Thomas Starr King, Boston (MA), 6–18; Charles Adam Smith, Easton (PA), 1852.

25. Charles Adam Smith, Easton (PA), 1852, 24–26; John G. Richardson, Lawrence (MA), 1852, 17. Cf. Blight, *Frederick Douglass*, 232–234.
26. Frederick Douglass, Rochester (NY), 1852, 4, 20.
27. Martha S. Jones, *Birthright Citizens: A History of Race and Rights in Antebellum America* (Cambridge University Press, 2018), ch. 2; F. R. Anspach, Hagerstown (MD), 1852, 4.
28. Frederick Douglass, Rochester (NY), 1852, 27–32. Douglass's hostility here was in inverse relationship to his prophetic hopes: see Blight, *Frederick Douglass*, 236–240.
29. I. N. Wyckoff, Albany (NY), 1852, 29–31.
30. James Sheldon, Buffalo (NY), 1852, 13; Frederick Douglass, Rochester (NY), 1852, 20–21. Richard T. Merrick, Baltimore (MD), 1852, 15, and Samuel Harris, Pittsfield (MA), 1852, 7–8, both offered positive comparisons of the United States to foreign places. Augustus Russell Pope, Somerville (MA), 1852, 4–5, 18, saw similarities between American slavery and oppressive regimes abroad.
31. Frederick Douglass, Rochester (NY), 1852, 38.
32. Samuel J. May, Jamestown (NY), 1856, 4.

Chapter 5. Revolution's End

1. Two years later, Richard Almgill Harrison, Pleasant Valley (OH), 1863, 3, reflected explicitly on the contrast between previous peacetime orations and the wartime ones.
2. Isaac Newton Wyckoff, Albany (NY), 1852, 10; Charles Anderson, Cincinnati (OH), 1855, 27, 29; Charles Edward Pickett, Sacramento (CA), 1857, 15. See also John L. Manning, Charleston (SC), 1848, 25; and C. J. W. Plowden, Watchesaw (SC), 1857, 13–15.
3. Joshua Sidney Henshaw, Utica (NY), 1848; William Whitwell Greenough, Boston (MA), 1849, 24–25. But see also William Law Learned, Newburgh (NY), 1855, 20–21, which suggests that Americans are failing.
4. Samuel A. Law, Stamford (NY), 1858; Samuel J. May, Jamestown (NY), 1856, 16. See also Edwin Hewes Tenney, Rome (TN),

1859, 12: "Let us repair then to these scenes with memorative gratitude."

5. "General Herr von Louis Kershoot," Greenfield (MA), 1859, 6–7, 5, 9.
6. "General Herr von Louis Kershoot," Greenfield (MA), 1859, 6–7.
7. Kenneth M. Stampp, *And the War Came: The North and the Secession Crisis, 1860–1861* (Louisiana State University Press, 1950), 69–86.
8. John R. Warner, Gettysburg (PA), 1861, 7; George Ticknor Curtis, Boston (MA), 1862, 42. Jordan Stokes, Nashville (TN), 1862, 6, on the other hand, thought the "present rebellion" would determine whether the "experiment of self-government" would be "successful."
9. John Jay, Mt. Kisco (NY), 1861, 3–4, 11–15; John R. Warner, Gettysburg (PA), 1861, 6. See also Sidney Dean, Providence (RI), 1864, 19 ("I hail the return of the old patriotism of 1776"); Samuel Lunt Caldwell, Providence (RI), 1861, 14, who saw the war as settling the question of whether the United States would be a "nation"; and George B. Loring, Salem (MA), 1862, 23, 29–30, which repeatedly linked revolutionary past and Civil War present.
10. Walter Clarke, Buffalo (NY), 1862, 11; Thomas Russell, Boston (MA), 1864, 12. Many orators invoked the military spirit of the revolutionary era as connected to or revived by the Union Army, including Charles E. Fitch, Delphi (NY), 1861, 11; and Dennis McMahon, New Rochelle (NY), 1862, 26–28.
11. Brainerd Kellogg, Middlebury (VT), 1866, 24. See also the similar approach by Walter Clarke, Buffalo (NY), 1862, 5–11, about the Civil War as a "second nativity" for the Republic.
12. G. D. Hill, Yankton (Dakota Terr.), 1864, in *Yankton Press and Dakotan*, July 9, 1864. The theme of slavery as a fatal error of the founding generation was a common one: Richard Busteed, Huntington (NY), 1862, 8 ("cancer"); Walter Clark, Buffalo (NY), 1862, 11–15 ("concealed . . . elements of ruin"); Theophilus Parsons, Boston (MA), 1861, 35 ("enormous mistake"); Oliver

Wendell Holmes, Boston (MA), 1863, 16–18. Another version of this argument, by Dennis McMahon, New Rochelle (NY), 1862, 18–19, argued that "of late years, our race of revolutionary patriots had ceased to exist" but that they were now being revived.

13. "Declaration of the Immediate Causes Which Induce and Justify the Secession of South Carolina from the Federal Union," December 24, 1860, https://avalon.law.yale.edu/19th_century/csa_scarsec.asp. Southern Fourth of July orators echoed the appropriation of the Revolution: see Alexander Watkins Terrell, Austin (TX), 1861, 8, 17, who made the Confederate States into a continuation of the revolutionary struggle against "despotism."
14. John Jay, Mt. Kisco (NY), 1861, 3–4, 11–15; Edward Everett, New York (NY), 1861, 8. The related need to legitimate Northern war aims lay behind the long self-justification in Oliver Wendell Holmes, Boston (MA), 1863, 25–34. The Democrat William Corry, Canton (OH), 1863, 10–16, on the other hand, gave the counterarguments justifying Southern secession a generous hearing.
15. Augustus Woodbury, Providence (RI), 1862, 11–13. See the similar attacks on Southerners for claiming a "justifiable revolution" in Richard Busteed, Huntington (NY), 1862, 3, as well as the play on the concept of "revolution" in George Ticknor Curtis, Boston (MA), 1862, 17, 38.
16. Augustus Woodbury, Providence (RI), 1862, 13–14, 18–19.
17. Jordan Stokes, Nashville (TN), 1862, 8; Orville Hickman Browning, Quincy (IL), 1863, 5; Samuel Kirkland Lothrop, Boston (MA), 1866, 10. See also Charles A. Sumner, Great Barrington (MA), 1861, 6–8.
18. See Eric Foner, *Reconstruction: America's Unfinished Revolution, 1863–1877* (Harper & Row, 1988); and Manisha Sinha, *The Rise and Fall of the Second American Republic: Reconstruction, 1860–1920* (Liveright, 2024).
19. J. W. Hough, Santa Barbara (CA), 1873, in *Santa Barbara Press*, July 12, 1873; L. H. Gulick, Honolulu (HI), 1865, in *Pacific Commercial Advertiser*, July 8, 1865.

20. Data from *Fourth of July Orations Database*.
21. B. B. French, Washington (DC), 1870, in *The Evening Star* (Washington, DC), July 5, 1870; D. H. Chamberlain, Columbia (SC), 1871, 13; William Everett, Boston (MA), 1870, 7.
22. Charles Francis Adams, Quincy (MA), 1869, 4. This coincidence was mentioned as well by B. B. French, Washington (DC), 1870.
23. On commemorations, see David W. Blight, *Race and Reunion: The Civil War in American Memory* (Harvard University Press, 2003), 65–73; and Mitch Kachun, *Festivals of Freedom: Memory and Meaning in African American Emancipation, 1808–1915* (University of Massachusetts Press, 2003), chs. 3 and 4. George B. Loring, Salem (MA), 1868, *Daily Journal* (Boston), July 6, 1868.
24. John G. Brown, Jamestown (OH), 1866, *Christian Recorder*, July 29, 1866.
25. William Everett, Boston (MA), 1870, 5–6.
26. William Everett, Boston (MA), 1870, 12–13.
27. William Everett, Boston (MA), 1870, 26, 31, 34–38.
28. "Charleston Correspondence," *Christian Recorder*, July 15, 1865.
29. Captain Chapman, "A Republican Fourth of July Festival at Carrollton," 1868, *New Orleans Advocate*, July 11, 1868.
30. John G. Brown, Jamestown (OH), 1866, *Christian Recorder*, July 29, 1866.
31. John G. Brown, Jamestown (OH), 1866, *Christian Recorder*, July 29, 1866.

Chapter 6. Aftershocks

1. Franklin D. Roosevelt, Hyde Park (NY), 1941, http://www.fdr library.marist.edu/_resources/images/msf/msf01435.
2. Ralph Ingersoll Lockwood, New York (NY), 1829, 3. C. Edwards Lester, Great Barrington (MA), 1849, 2, promised that he would be "so brief . . . you can hardly have time to get tired before I have done."
3. See *Oxford English Dictionary*, "centenary" and "centennial." Both attest the usage, referring to a hundredth anniversary, as dating to the seventeenth century. But the usage expanded in

the late eighteenth century and only became truly widespread in the nineteenth century.

4. Michael D. Hattem, *The Memory of '76: The Revolution in American History* (Yale University Press, 2024), 103–105; *Centennial Guide of the Exposition and Philadelphia* (Magee & Son, 1876), 62–63.
5. "Joint resolution on the celebration of the Centennial in the several counties, March 13, 1876," *Statutes at Large* 19:211. For the proclamations, see Henry Clay Platt, Huntington (NY), 1876, 3–4.
6. For evidence that contemporaries were aware of a change in tone and content, see Howard Hastings Martin, "Orations on the Anniversary of American Independence, 1777–1876" (PhD diss., Northwestern University, 1955), 328–329.
7. The *Fourth of July Orations Database* contains 12 entries for 1875 and 161 entries for 1876 (including four in foreign or unknown locations), a more than 13-fold increase. Other digital catalogs show similar changes of magnitude. The Harvard Library catalog, HOLLIS, lists 6 orations for 1875 and 76 for 1876, while HathiTrust shows 7 orations for 1875 and 64 for 1876.
8. Henry Clay Platt, Huntington (NY), 1876.
9. Henry Clay Platt, Huntington (NY), 1876, 10.
10. John Crowell, Haverhill (MA), 1876, 13–18, 9–10; Samuel Greene Arnold, Providence (RI), 1876.
11. William F. M. Arny, Santa Fe (NM), 1876, 14–33, 7; Lawrence R. Murphy, *Frontier Crusader—William F. M. Arny* (Tucson: University of Arizona Press, 1972).
12. See Ned Blackhawk, *The Rediscovery of America: Native Peoples and the Unmaking of U.S. History* (Yale University Press, 2023), ch. 11, esp. 367–368; and Kathleen DuVal, *Native Nations: A Millenium in North America* (Random House, 2024), ch. 12.
13. Ellen Carol Dubois, *Suffrage: Women's Long Battle for the Vote* (Simon & Schuster, 2020), chs. 2 and 3. See also Martha S. Jones, *Vanguard: How Black Women Broke Barriers, Won the Vote, and Insisted on Equality for All* (Basic Books, 2020), ch. 5.
14. "Speech of Mrs. Belva A. Lockwood, July 4th," *The Ballot Box*, August 1876.

15. [Matilda Joslyn Gage,] "The Ladies' Revolution," *The Ballot Box*, September 1876.
16. "Speech of Mrs. Sara J. Spencer, July 4th," *The Ballot Box*, August 1876.
17. Le Baron Colt, Boston (MA), 1905, 1–2, 5. This is in part a quotation from James Bryce, *The American Commonwealth* (emphasis mine).
18. "A Rancher Speaks to His Neighbors . . . July 4, 1886," in *Theodore Roosevelt Association Journal* 3:2 (Summer 1977): 6–7; Henry F. Pringle, *Theodore Roosevelt: A Biography* (Harcourt, Brace, 1931), 166, 206; *Address of President Taft at Marion, Ind.*, 62 Cong. 1st sess., Senate, Doc 79; Woodrow Wilson, Mount Vernon (VA), 1918; Eugene Debs, Chicago (IL), 1901.
19. Theodore Roosevelt, Huntington (NY), 1903.
20. Woodrow Wilson, Mount Vernon (VA), 1918, 3–4.
21. Eugene Debs, Chicago (IL), 1901.
22. Josiah Quincy, Boston (MA), 1891, 9, 43–44.
23. James Beck, Philadelphia (PA), 1893, 9, 7, 11.
24. For a detailed discussion of the Fourth in this period, in a local context, see Mary Lou Nemanic, *One Day for Democracy* (Ohio, 2007), 70–74. A 1915 celebration she discusses included an oration, but it does not seem to have been the main focus of the event.
25. Calvin Coolidge, Philadelphia (PA), 1926: See https://www.presidency.ucsb.edu/documents/address-the-celebration-the-150th-anniversary-the-declaration-independence-philadelphia.
26. HOLLIS shows only a single oration published in 1926: the official Boston oration. See Andrew James Peters, Boston (MA), 1926.
27. Franklin Delano Roosevelt, Monticello (VA), 1936: https://www.monticello.org/exhibits-events/calendar-of-events/july-4-at-monticello/july-4th-speakers-at-monticello/fdr-july-4-1936-at-monticello/.

28. Harry S. Truman, Washington (DC), 1951: https://www.trumanlibrary.gov/library/public-papers/144/address-ceremonies-commemorating-175th-anniversary-declaration.
29. John F. Kennedy, Philadelphia (PA), 1962: https://www.jfklibrary.org/learn/about-jfk/historic-speeches/address-at-independence-hall.
30. Hattem, *Memory of '76*, 252–264. Established by Public Law, 89–491, July 4, 1966.
31. Robert Hartmann, "Memorandum," June 10, 1976, in box 67, folder "Fourth of July (1976)—Bicentennial Speeches: General (2)," John Marsh Files, Gerald R. Ford Presidential Library, Ann Arbor, MI.
32. David Gergen, "America—A Continuing Experiment," ibid.
33. Irving Kristol to Hartmann, June 7, 1976, ibid.
34. Robert Hartmann, "Memorandum," June 10, 1976, ibid.
35. David Gergen, "Memorandum," July 1, 1976, ibid.

Epilogue

1. See the excellent discussion of US empire in Daniel Immerwahr, *How to Hide an Empire: A History of the Greater United States* (Farrar, Straus and Giroux, 2019), 6–35. On European empire, see esp. David Todd, *A Velvet Empire: French Informal Imperialism in the Nineteenth Century* (Princeton University Press, 2021), 16–24; and Mary D. Lewis, *Divided Rule: Sovereignty and Empire in French Tunisia, 1881–1938* (University of California Press, 2014).
2. The nineteenth-century version of this argument is well represented by George Bancroft, whose *History of the United States of America* (Little, Brown, 1854–1860) advanced a notion of unified peoplehood. This has been echoed recently by J. D. Vance: see his speech at the Claremont Institute, July 5, 2025, particularly his critique of so-called creedal nationalism. These views have been vigorously opposed by a more multiculturalist approach, which thinks in terms of diverse "peoples" coexisting in a single political unit without either melding or assimilating.

3. The alleged conservatism of the American Revolution has been a leitmotif since Frederick Gentz, *The Origin and Principles of the American Revolution Compared with the Origin and Principles of the French Revolution*, trans. John Quincy Adams (Philadelphia, 1800). It figured, in different ways, in both Louis Hartz, *The Liberal Tradition in America: An Interpretation of American Political Thought Since the Revolution* (Harcourt, Brace, 1955), 67–70 and passim; and Hannah Arendt, *On Revolution* (Viking, 1963), 24–25, 55–58.

Appendix

1. William B. Sprague, *Annals of the American Pulpit* (Carter & Brothers, 1959), 1:666.

INDEX

Credit: Laura Stevens

Nathan Perl-Rosenthal is professor of history, French and Italian, and law at the University of Southern California. His writing has appeared in *The Wall Street Journal*, *The Atlantic*, *The Nation*, and the *Los Angeles Times*. The award-winning author of *The Age of Revolutions* and *Citizen Sailors*, he lives in Los Angeles and Cambridge, Massachusetts.

RAISING READERS

Books Build Bright Futures

Thank you for reading this book and for being a reader of books in general. We are so grateful to share being part of a community of readers with you, and we hope you will join us in passing our love of books on to the next generation of readers.

Did you know that reading for enjoyment is the single biggest predictor of a child's future happiness and success?

More than family circumstances, parents' educational background, or income, reading impacts a child's future academic performance, emotional well-being, communication skills, economic security, ambition, and happiness.

Studies show that kids reading for enjoyment in the US is in rapid decline:

- In 2012, 53% of 9-year-olds read almost every day. Just 10 years later, in 2022, the number had fallen to 39%.
- In 2012, 27% of 13-year-olds read for fun daily. By 2023, that number was just 14%.

TOGETHER, WE CAN COMMIT TO **RAISING READERS** AND CHANGE THIS TREND.

HOW?

- Read to children in your life daily.
- Model reading as a fun activity.
- Reduce screen time.
- Start a family, school, or community book club.
- Visit bookstores and libraries regularly.
- Listen to audiobooks.
- Read the book before you see the movie.
- Encourage your child to read aloud to a pet or stuffed animal.
- Give books as gifts.
- Donate books to families and communities in need.

Books build bright futures, and **Raising Readers** is our shared responsibility.

For more information, visit JoinRaisingReaders.com

Sources: National Endowment for the Arts, National Assessment of Educational Progress, WorldBookDay.com, Nielsen BookData's 2023 "Understanding the Children's Book Consumer"